A Parable of Fate

The Servant, The Vizier
& The Flying Baker

written by
Ibtesam Ismail

Cover Art and Illustrations: OoO studios Ltd

Proofreading: Annam Ahmad

Book design and typesetting by Lunetta Osterhaus

Edited by Yasin Chines

First Edition

123456789

ISBN 978-1-0681606-0-8

Dedication

For those who feel they have fallen short of their potential.

This story is fiction.
It won't offer you all the answers.

But if it brings you a moment of peace, a smile or a new perspective,
then it's done what I hoped.

You are still on your journey.
And as long as you keep striving towards righteousness,
your potential is not lost.

Remember God often,
and He will guide you towards the purpose He placed in you from the start.

A smooth sea never made a skilled sailor.

–Popularized by Franklin D. Roosevelt,
from an African Proverb

Contents

Part III: Rising Together

Part IV: As it was Meant

A Parable of Fate

*The Servant, The Vizier &
The Flying Baker*

Part I

Before the Sky Fell

I

Kingdoms do not fall when kings die; they fall when ty-
rants rise. Beneath the honey-gold sun and clear
blue sky, nestled in a lush valley flanked by two towering
mountains, lay Al-Waadi – a city of resilience and beauty.
It stood proudly on both banks of the mighty Horn River,
a shimmering ribbon of liquid silver that carved through
the heart of the land. Under the wise and beloved rule of
their Sultan, the people of Al-Waadi lived with purpose
and contentment. The city thrived, its vibrancy as rich and
varied as the colours of its bustling marketplace.

In the winding, cobbled streets, children played freely, their laughter ringing out like music between the stone
walls of homes and shops. Young and old moved through
the city with purpose. Faces lit with warmth and genuine
smiles. Neighbours greeted one another in passing with
affection and ease. Along the river's edge, fishermen cast

their nets into the shimmering waters, gathering the river's abundant gifts to feed their families.

The marketplace was a world of its own, alive with the scents of spices, ripe fruit, and the rich, earthy aroma of freshly baked bread. Vendors proudly displayed their goods to passersby. The air buzzed with energy; voices engaged in friendly barter. A skilled artisan showcased intricately designed pottery, while nearby, a merchant's vibrant silk scarves fluttered like banners in the gentle breeze. Every street and home seemed to hum with a quiet joy.

For now, Al-Waadi was at peace.

But peace is never still – it only pretends to be. Peace, as they all knew, is a treasure hard-won but kept only with care. Though it shields the kingdom like a mighty wall, even the smallest crack can invite chaos. Peace is a flame that must be tended. If ignored, it can vanish with a single gust.

Maintaining this harmony demands a careful balance between justice and mercy, freedom and security, and power and accountability – each resting on either side of the scale. Those who uphold this balance must be without corruption, for any blemish in their character can tip the scales and disrupt the delicate equilibrium that sustains peace. When the guardians of this harmony falter, the entire kingdom feels the tremor.

Within the palace walls, where power and ambition entwined, a tale began to take shape, one that would come to be known as the Parable of Fate. The kingdom's greatest threat was not an invading army or outside force; it was a danger that had been allowed to take root within the Sultan's own palace. As the Sultan's years advanced, an unsettling truth loomed: he had no heir to succeed him. In the shadows, the Sultan's Vizier, a cunning man named Ra'ees, concealed his own dark ambitions. Once a trusted advisor, the Vizier's internal peace had long been eroded by greed, envy, and selfish desire. His ambitions grew quietly, like a shadow lengthening at dusk – subtle yet undeniable, unnoticed until it was too late.

Though the kingdom flourished under their rule, the Vizier believed his contributions to the kingdom's prosperity went unnoticed. Why was it always the Sultan who was praised, adored and celebrated? Could the kingdom have thrived as it did without his guidance and expertise?

Blinded by his pride, he failed to see the truth. It was the Sultan's restraint, not the Vizier's ambition, that ensured Al-Waadi's stability. Their success had been forged through partnership, yet the Vizier saw only his own reflection in every triumph.

When a pocket of rebels began causing turmoil in a distant corner of the kingdom, the short-tempered Vizier's fury was immediate. His face turned red, as he stormed into the council chamber. With a thunderous slam of his fist on the table, he sent papers and goblets trembling.

"We must crush these rebels with the full might of the kingdom!" he bellowed, his voice booming through the chamber. Yet, as always, the final decision lay with the Sultan.

Instead of adopting the Vizier's militant approach, the Sultan opted for diplomacy, dispatching an emissary to persuade the rebels to stand down. He believed negotiation should always be the first course of action. This choice, although wise and measured, only deepened the Vizier's resentment.

Though he commanded authority over those beneath him – in the Sultan's presence – he was reduced to a shadow. His frustration festered, swelling his sense of self-importance to dangerous heights. Despite his short stature, the Vizier's ego had outgrown him. He saw himself as superior, even to the Sultan. Seething with anger, he stormed through the palace courtyard, his strides aggressive and defiant. Each furious step tore into the emerald grass as if trying to uproot the very earth beneath him.

"Vizier! Does this title even carry any weight?" he grumbled, pacing the emerald patches like a caged lion. His voice dripped with resentment as his words clawed at the empty air.

"My honour, my respect, my words – meaningless the moment the Sultan enters the room." His anger simmered, spilling into a bitter tirade.

"A taunt! A deception! A title draped in gold but hollow, with no real power. What good is a shepherd to a lion?"

"If a lion yearns to roam free, can a mere shepherd reign it back in? Would a lion bow and allow anyone to dictate how it rules its domain? Never! So why must I be shackled by this Sultan's whims?" His pacing quickened, his irritation boiling over.

"My abilities far surpass these confining walls, yet here I am, chained by loyalty and duty, a prisoner in golden cuffs. Every victory belongs to me just as much as to him, yet it is the Sultan who basks in the glory, hailed as the hero of the realm." He spat the words; his fists clenched at his sides.

"Why must he continue to undermine my counsel, to overshadow my triumphs?"

"Perhaps the Sultan seeks to humiliate me, to make me look inadequate in front of our people. Every choice he makes, each fleeting glance, feels like a calculated move in some invisible game."

"And when he finally casts me from this high perch, no one will dare question him. They'll celebrate him – the noble leader who saved the kingdom from my supposed tyranny."

"But the truth is clear: he fears me."

"He fears my ambition, my intellect. It eats away at him like rust corrodes iron, eroding his confidence bit by bit. Why else would he undermine my every suggestion?"

"It's as though he wants me to bow, to dance to his tune, to show the kingdom that I am nothing without him. But I am a lion, not a puppet! I will not dangle on his strings, waiting for him to pull the threads of my destiny."

"No."

"A lion doesn't wait for permission to roar. A lion seizes the moment and claims its rightful place as king. And so shall I." He clenched his jaw, the fire in his heart igniting darker, more dangerous thoughts.

"As the sailors say, the fall of a tidal wave is more destructive than its rise. Should he push me to the edge, I will unleash my fury, leaving nothing but ruin in my wake! I have served long enough to know my worth, and it is time the Sultan recognised that I am not a pawn to be toyed with. He will see – whether he wishes to or not..."

His mind raced and arrogance swelled, feeding the storm of ambition brewing within. Like a tempest ready to erupt, the Vizier began to plot his next move, the shadow of his desires consuming him whole.

II

Adjacent to the opulent grand palace stood the modest servants' quarters, a humble complex of four sections surrounding a small courtyard. A shared wall, adorned with wooden walnut arched doors, connected the palace to this quieter domain, creating a passage between two vastly different worlds. The other three sides of the courtyard featured old colonnaded galleries, their arches framing the dormitories where the servants resided.

As dusk settled over Al-Waadi, the courtyard came alive with activity. Many servants prepared for rest, retreating to their quarters, while others lingered in small groups. They exchanged stories and laughter, reliving moments of the day. Leaning against a column, a young servant sat with his head buried in a book, occasionally adjusting his position to catch the fading daylight on his pages.

His name was Zayd.

A man in his early twenties, slender yet strong, with a quiet presence that naturally drew attention. His sharp yet gentle features were framed by tousled dark hair that fell loosely over his brow. He looked like someone who carried out his duties without complaint – steady, reliable.

But the depth of his brown eyes hinted at something unresolved, an inner struggle he carried in silence. For Zayd, reading was more than a pastime; it was an escape – a refuge from the restless cloud that had settled over his life. Like water trapped in a bucket drawn from a rushing river, he felt confined, stagnant. Once, his life had moved with promise. Now, it drifted.

Why? Why did this unease persist after years of dedicated service? Was it arrogant of him to want more, or were his skills and knowledge truly being wasted here?

Al-Waadi thrived, yet Zayd couldn't ignore the quiet ache that pulled at him. Each passing moment forced him to question whether he was meant for more. His reality had fallen short of the ambitions that once drove him. His father had been one of the kingdom's success stories. Trade had prospered. Wealth followed. Then fate intervened.

Death came without warning, leaving behind a grieving widow and an infant son. Despite her sorrow, Zayd's mother poured more love into the four chambers of his heart than they could contain. Though she inherited a comfortable fortune, she lived simply, dedicating her resources towards his future.

Under the guidance of Al-Waadi's finest teachers, Zayd flourished. He absorbed every lesson, every principle. Justice. Truth. Honour. He dreamed of standing in the Sultan's court as a judge – a beacon of fairness.

His mother's unwavering support fuelled this ambition. Like a candle burning itself away to illuminate his path, she sacrificed her own comforts to ensure he had the best chance at success. But just as Zayd's star began to rise, his mother's health began to decline. Her strength waned like a tide retreating into a horizon it would never cross again, and soon, even the simplest tasks became a struggle.

When that day came, Zayd did not hesitate – he set aside his studies to care for her, believing that his love and discipline would be enough. But no amount of devotion could hold back time. He remained by her side in her final moments, holding her hand as the warmth of her spirit slowly faded.

The candle that lit his world went out – and Zayd was left in darkness.

The world rarely sings the praise of great mothers. Yet it is so often they who carve the path boys walk to become men. With their quiet strength, though often unseen, they lay each stone of the road that leads to greatness. Zayd's mother was one such woman – a silent architect of his dreams, a steady force shaping the man he was destined to become.

Her love had enveloped him like a warm embrace. The vibrant colours of his childhood had dimmed to muted grey. In his moments of solitude, Zayd found himself sinking into a well of sorrow, drawing from it endlessly, yet never quenching the thirst of his grief. Each drop of heartache sank deeper into him, clinging like a shadow that refused to fade. Only now did Zayd grasp how precious their bond had been. Without it, the world had no shape. The absence of his mother's love left more than an ache in his heart – it opened a wound in his soul. For it is the soul that bleeds when the heart is given no love to kindle.

The only escape from his sorrow was to return to his studies, a pursuit of progress and clarity. Yet fate had charted a different course. The cost of his mother's care had drained the wealth he had inherited, leaving him with nothing but the weight of his grief. With no money and his dreams slipping through his fingers, Zayd had little choice but to seek refuge in the only place that could offer him work, food, and a semblance of stability: the Sultan's palace.

It was a bitter irony. He had once envisioned himself seated among the Sultan's council, imparting wisdom as a judge, a role of respect and authority. Instead, he now wore the humble robes of a servant. Yet, even in this role, Zayd held onto hope. Perhaps serving within those grand walls would one day lead him to the path he had long dreamed of. He believed that his proximity to the court might offer him the knowledge and experience needed to rise above his station.

"ZAYD!"

The Vizier burst through the wooden arched doors of the servants' quarter, still simmering with anger from his earlier confrontation with the Sultan.

Zayd was steady. Efficient. Diligent. Word spread. In time, he became head servant. He felt like a sailor at sea, bound by duty, yet his heart remained ashore – left behind with the dreams he could no longer afford to chase. In the grandeur of the palace – the very heart of the kingdom, where its fate was shaped – Zayd moved like a shadow, unnoticed amid the pulse of power. While others ascended, their ambitions igniting in every hall and chamber, he remained a quiet presence, tethered to a life that had veered far from the path he once imagined.

Time slipped past him like sand through an hourglass, each grain carrying away a fragment of the dreams he once held so fiercely. He began to see how easily dreams could dissolve under the weight of responsibility and how quietly passion could die. Each day, his imagined future drifted further away, until only echoes of it remained. The Vizier's eyes burned with urgency.

"Come. Now."

Zayd leapt to his feet, instinctively straightening as the powerful man loomed before him. He had no idea that beneath the vast starlit sky, fate had already begun to stir – and that from this night forward everything would change.

III

"Respected Vizier," Zayd said *with a slight nod, brushing back* his hair and instinctively straightening his shirt. He tried to appear composed despite the intensity radiating from the man before him.

"You may think I have come to you because the Sultan holds you in high regard," the Vizier said, his words laced with contempt. Zayd, ever eager to serve, felt a spark of hope ignite within him. Perhaps his diligence had finally been recognised. But the spark died quickly.

"No," the Vizier continued.

"I am here for two reasons. First, my duties at the palace prevent me from handling this matter myself – time is not on my side. And second…" He leaned in, his eyes narrowing like a predator sizing up its prey.

"You are the only servant who has not failed me. At least…not yet." The Vizier's eyes locked on Zayd; a flicker of disdain slipped through the cracks of his rigid expression.

How unfortunate, he thought, that he had to entrust this task to a mere servant. Zayd's heart sank. The glimmer of pride he had felt moments ago vanished, replaced by unease. The presence of the Vizier loomed like a storm cloud. Zayd stood frozen, unaware of the darker storm brewing within the man before him.

"Time is slipping," the Vizier pressed.

"And I require unwavering obedience. My patience wears thin, and I will not tolerate delays. Do you grasp the importance of what I'm entrusting to you?"

"Yes, respected Vizier. I am ready." Zayd nodded with conviction despite the faint tremble in his voice. Something about tonight was different. There was a strangeness in the Vizier's manner – a quiet tension hanging behind his words. An instinctive warning. Zayd couldn't shake the feeling that this was no ordinary errand. Something else was at play; something covered in secrecy. Zayd felt a chill settle across him. Even the Vizier, for all his authority, seemed wary of revealing too much. The man's gaze bore into Zayd, pinning him into place, fuelling his confusion.

What could be so important that it demanded such secrecy?

And more importantly – was he capable of fulfilling the task?

"Take this!" The Vizier thrust a rolled map against Zayd's chest, hard enough to knock the breath from him. With a swift flick of his wrist, the Vizier unfurled the map. The sound of parchment crackled in the tense air. He traced a route with his finger, stopping at a jagged mark near the edge of the page.

"You will journey to this cave," he said, tapping the map. "There, you'll retrieve a pouch. You'll know it when you see it." Zayd's confusion burned beneath the surface, but he knew better than to question the Vizier. He gave a firm nod, heart racing.

"Yes, respected Vizier. I will do as you command." A glint of frustration crossed the Vizier's face.

"My urgency does not mean I am softening my expectations. This task requires precision and discretion. You'd better move quickly – for time is of the essence. If you linger, you may not find what I seek." Zayd nodded again, trying to keep his expression steady, but the Vizier wasn't finished. Perhaps to assert his dominance, or simply because his anger slipped past his control. Without warning, he pounced.

He yanked Zayd forward, twisting his fingers into the fabrics of Zayd's shirt. His grip allowed no escape. Their faces were inches apart. Like a hawk, his eyes tracked every flicker of movement.

"Remember Zayd," he hissed.

"Not a soul is to hear of this assignment. Should even a whisper escape your lips, the consequences will be unforgettable." His fingers tightened, pressing the threat into Zayd's very bones.

"Do you understand?"

"Yes, Vizier. I... understand." Zayd swallowed.

"Good." The Vizier released him abruptly.

"Three days, Zayd. Fail me, and you'll learn the true meaning of regret." He warned and then turned on his heel and strode away, his cloak billowing in his wake. Zayd remained rooted in place, chest tight, map clutched in his hand. The questions circled him like vultures. What had he just agreed to?

IV

*The next morning, before the sun had fully risen, Zayd gath-*ered his provisions, tucking away a battered book alongside his meagre supplies. He paused in the doorway of the servants' quarters, his fingers tightening around the strap of his satchel. The cool morning air carried the scent of damp earth and morning mist – sharp and alive – it made him shiver. Whether from the cold or the thought of what lay ahead, he couldn't tell.

This was no ordinary errand. In his mind, he replayed the Vizier's harsh words, a warning that still bothered him. This was no simple task, of that he was certain. But why him? And what was the Vizier not saying?

He knew little of what awaited him, yet the burden of it pressed upon him already – a responsibility that felt both momentous and unnerving. For if he failed, it would mean more than just the Vizier's wrath. It could shatter the new world he had just begun to know.

With a final glance back at the servants' quarters, Zayd braced himself for the journey ahead – unaware that the kingdom of Al-Waadi's fate and perhaps his own, hung dangerously in the balance. He set off along the narrow dirt path, his footsteps crunching over dew-laden grass, carrying him beyond the palace walls and into the vast, waiting unknown.

As he travelled towards the marked location, Zayd was struck by the sheer beauty of the kingdom – a beauty he had seldom stopped to truly see. He plucked ripe berries from the brambles, their sweetness lingering on his tongue, and sipped from the crystal-clear waters of the majestic Horn River. The meadows stretched endlessly, bursting with vibrant wildflowers in shades of amber, gold, crimson, and violet, each colour adding to the beauty of the landscape. For a fleeting moment, surrounded by nature's splendour, he allowed himself a moment to forget the burden of his mission.

But the weight of the Vizier's words lingered still, a shadow trailing his every step.

After what felt like significant progress, Zayd paused to catch his breath – not for his body's sake, but for something deeper, harder to name. At times, his own thoughts became unsettling, and to escape their stress, he would reach for his book, delving into the stories it held. Each familiar tale wrapped around him like a comforting blanket. Each narrative transported him to distant lands and legendary heroes – allowing him to momentarily escape his own reality, if only for a while.

In Al-Waadi, as the cold season approached, the kingdom braced itself for weeks of relentless storms. Fierce winds howled through the streets. The heavens poured without mercy. And yet, the people welcomed this time of year. There was a strange sense of comfort in watching the tempest rage from the safety of their homes, wrapped in warmth while nature unleashed its fury outside.

Perhaps it was the reminder that while the elements raged, they remained protected and secure – a realisation that filled their hearts with gratitude. Would they feel the same way if the sky's tears soaked them, if the unstable winds pounded them without mercy?

Probably not. Comfort is a privilege of the sheltered. Zayd, too, found solace in the stories of others – tales of hardship and hope, where struggle always led somewhere, where meaning emerged from chaos.

They let him pretend, even for a while, that everything was unfolding as it should. That he was on a path carved by destiny, not thrown into the current by someone else's will. Each story became a gentle deception. Not to blind him, but to give him just enough light to keep walking.

And still, he walked.

Finally, as the sun dipped below the horizon, casting a golden glow over the landscape, Zayd reached the foot of a towering mountain. Its jagged silhouette was carved against the fiery sky – an ominous presence that loomed before him.

The air grew cooler. A breeze stirred through the trees, rustling leaves like whispers trading secrets. He could feel it – the shift, the unspoken pull towards something fateful.

At the mountain's base lay the cave he sought, its entrance shrouded in an eerie darkness that seemed to swallow the last rays of sunlight. Yet, from somewhere deep within, a faint flicker of light emerged – a distant glow, like a lone star fighting against the night.

He stood at the threshold, the silence pressing in around him. For a moment, he did nothing but breathe – slow deliberate breaths to steady the anxious rhythm of his heart. Then he stepped forward, into the darkness. The air was thick with the pungent smell of smoke and unfamiliar herbs, a strong mix that filled his lungs and set his senses on edge. His shadow twisted and stretched along the jagged walls, morphing with each flicker of light from deep within, as though the darkness itself sought to ensnare him.

It felt less like entering a cave and more like stepping across the edge of the world – into something he might never return from. A growling voice rumbled through the depths.

"Who dares enter my domain?" The words reverberated around him, shaking the very walls, as if the cave itself had spoken. Zayd tensed, his breath catching in his throat. His mind raced.

Was this the voice of some forgotten creature? A towering giant?

Perhaps a beast with horns like forged blades and eyes like molten gold.

Perhaps it would lunge from the shadows, rip him apart before he could even speak.

The silence that followed was almost worse than the voice itself. Whatever lay ahead, he had no choice but to face it.

"I...I mean no harm." Then, from the gloom, emerged a figure. Not a monster. Not a man-eating beast.

Just... a man. Old, hunched and wrapped in a threadbare robe that looked stitched together from several others, none of which matched. His beard was wild and grey, though not long enough to be noble. His face, deeply lined, wore the expression of quiet mystery – whether from years of solitude or too many years in the shadows, Zayd couldn't tell.

He didn't speak at first. Just stared. Zayd blinked, unsure if he was supposed to bow or speak or kneel.

"Er... I'm Zayd," he offered. "I've been sent by the Vizier."

"Hmm?" the old man grunted. Zayd raised his voice.

"Ra'ees, the Vizier of Al-Waadi." At that, the man nodded – slowly, as though the name stirred a distant memory he'd nearly forgotten. He straightened his back a little, then winced as something clicked in protest. He tried to mask it by adjusting his robe, which only made it fall off one shoulder. He yanked it back up with as much dignity as he could muster.

"Ah. The Vizier," he said at last. "Yes, yes. I thought he might send someone. Eventually." He let out a dry, rasping cough, the sound bouncing eerily off the stone walls. Zayd blinked.

Was this the man the Vizier had sent him to? This frail, weathered figure who looked as though a strong breeze might carry him away.

He vanished into the darkness for a moment, then returned cradling a small leather pouch with the kind of care one might reserve for an ancient relic. He turned back to Zayd and held it aloft, letting it dangle between his fingers.

"This... this is what the Vizier sent you for."

"It holds power... great power." Zayd stared at it. It looked...ordinary. The kind sold by street vendors for a handful of coins. Whatever ancient power it supposedly held wasn't exactly radiating from its worn edges. The old man noticed the doubt in Zayd's face. He cleared his throat, straightened his back, and deepened his voice in a theatrical attempt at gravitas.

"Its power is not... obvious. But rest assured, the Vizier would not have sent you unless the matter was of grave importance."

Zayd said nothing. But inwardly, something shifted. Was this man truly a wielder of ancient knowledge? Or simply a relic of forgotten importance, trying to convince the world – and himself – that he still mattered?

Powers? he thought, wondering if he had missed something in the Vizier's instructions.

"Yes, yes." The old man continued, waving a frail hand dismissively. "Only those wise enough... or perhaps foolish enough... dare open it." He leaned in, his eyes glinting with an unsettling excitement.

"Would you like me to show you what's inside of it?"

If what this old man says is true, then he *definitely doesn't look wise enough – and I don't want to be foolish enough to look inside.* Zayd thought. Zayd hesitated, torn between curious and wary.

"The Vizier never mentioned I should... open it."

"Of course not!" The old man clutched the pouch to his chest, as if scandalised by the very idea – the same idea he had just suggested.

"Yes, you are right." Then, with a conspiratorial whisper, he added, "I would demonstrate its power, but... alas, I must conserve my strength."

Zayd nodded, though there was a flicker in his eyes that said, Sure. Whatever you say. He extended his hand to take the pouch, hoping to end the encounter quickly. The man, however, hesitated, gripping the pouch a moment too long – almost as if letting it go meant surrendering the last shred of importance he possessed.

His face shifted into what he clearly believed was a solemn expression.

"Handle it carefully," he said. "One day, you may look back on this and finally understand its true power." Zayd, torn between the urge to laugh and the urge to flee, forced a solemn nod.

"Thank you. I… won't forget." The old man returned the nod, clearly basking in his own imagined importance. As Zayd turned to leave, the man called out.

"And tell the Vizier… I made the poison myself…"

"Poison!" Zayd repeated, spinning around.

The old man froze. His eyes widened in delayed horror. He dropped his head into his hands, fingers pressing into his temple.

"Potion," he corrected.

"Yes, yes. Potion. A slip nothing more." He turned his back, busying himself with rearranging a few empty clay pots – pots that clearly hadn't been moved in months. His movements were restless, distracted. Under his breath, barely more than a whisper to himself, he muttered,

"Fool. Always one word too many…" Zayd couldn't quite make out the words, but the old man's tone had changed – quieter, rougher, as if arguing with some unseen version of himself. Then, with a loud clearing of his throat, he straightened, fixing his robe with unnecessary care and gesturing vaguely towards the mouth of the cave.

"Safe journey to you," he said with sudden formality, as though the encounter had gone precisely as planned.

Zayd stepped out into the cool night air, leaving the old man – and his muttered nonsense – behind. The absurdity of the man's theatrics momentarily distracted him from the reality of his task, but now, with the pouch tucked into his satchel, the weight of his duty settled firmly on his shoulders.

The Vizier hadn't merely sent him on an errand – he had sent him to a magician. A figure of secrecy and forbidden knowledge. A man cloaked not in wisdom, but in secrecy. In whispers. In fear. Despite the old man's frailty, Zayd couldn't ignore the significance of the Vizier's choice.

The kingdom had a long, troubled history with men like that. The power they wielded rarely brought anything but trouble. They weren't healers or guides – they were manipulators, architects of deception who bent fate to their will, leaving devastation in their wake. For the Vizier to seek out one of these figures, it meant that whatever he had planned was as dangerous as it was deliberate.

A faint shiver coursed through Zayd as he recalled the Vizier's instructions: Bring this directly to me. Do not, under any circumstances, open it. The pouch was small, unassuming – but its purpose was anything but. He had overheard hushed rumours before, of potions brewed in secrecy, of poisons designed to silence enemies, weaken allies, topple rulers.

This pouch was no mere charm or talisman. It was a weapon meant for the Sultan. A flurry of questions swirled in Zayd's mind, each more unsettling than the last.

Had he truly just stood before a magician – one of those shadowed figures spoken of in hushed warnings? And why would the Vizier, of all people, send him to a wielder of such forbidden arts?

Nothing about this felt right. He clenched his jaw, staring out into the night. *Had he become a tool in someone else's scheme? A quiet hand moving a piece on a board he couldn't see?* The thought clawed at him – made him pause on the narrow path.

What if I walked away? What if I refuse?

Yet, despite the whisper urging him to abandon the task, another voice – one quieter, steadier – held him in place. For now, he could only hope. Hope that his suspicions were wrong. Hope that he was not destined to become an innocent accomplice in something dark, dangerous and irreversible.

He glanced once more over his shoulder, back towards the cave. The magician was nowhere in sight. Just darkness. Just silence. The wind stirred the trees. The pouch pressed cold against his side.

And Zayd walked on – not away from the danger, but into it.

V

As the first light of dawn spilled over the kingdom, Zayd felt a sense of renewal wash over him. The first rays of sunlight stretched across the cold earth like gentle fingers, awakening the world from its slumber. Each shaft of light seeped into his skin, filling him with warmth, energy, and urging him to start his day.

In the stillness of morning, Zayd contemplated the mystery of life. Here he was, a small figure in a vast sprawling universe, yet his existence carried weight. The same sun that warmed his skin and brightened his surroundings also illuminated the struggles and triumphs of countless others across Al-Waadi and beyond. The mountains, valleys, and rivers carried stories – of love, loss, and hope – whispering their timeless echoes through the land.

Today marked a new beginning, not just for Zayd, but for all who wandered the kingdom, blissfully unaware that their fates were being shaped in unseen ways. Small actions often carry far-reaching consequences, sending ripples beyond what the eye can see. The first light of morning is filled with promise and uncertainty, offering fresh opportunities and unforeseen challenges. Like an untamed horse, the day brims with wild potential, and it is our choices that take hold of the reins.

As he packed the last of his things and prepared to return to the palace, Zayd inhaled deeply. The air was crisp. Clean. Every breath felt like a gift, a reminder that with life came the power to change, to learn, to grow. He felt, at once, both small and profoundly significant. Because even in the vastness of this world every heartbeat carries meaning. Every voice, an imprint. And every morning, a chance to rewrite one's story.

Still, he pressed on. Though he hadn't forgotten something wasn't right. As the path curved gently towards the city, he paused at the edge of the Horn River, kneeling to splash its cold water onto his face. He drank deeply, letting the chill of it sharpen his senses.

Then he saw it.

A massive brown bear, prowling the opposite bank. Its heavy paws disturbed the stones with each step, its shadow stretching long across the rippling surface of the water.

Zayd froze.

The distance between them wasn't far. One wrong move, and –

He ducked behind a tree. Panic surged, sharp and breathless. His pulse thundered. Then, spotting a low, sturdy branch overhead, he scrambled up it without thinking, lodging himself in the crook of its limbs. The bark bit into his palms. His breath caught in his throat.

The bear lumbered on. Sniffing the air. Then, with a soft grunt, it turned away, disappearing into the thickets. Zayd didn't move. He stayed still. Very still. Only when he was sure the bear had gone did he shift to climb down.

And that's when everything turned.

His foot caught a slick patch of bark. The branch cracked. And Zayd tumbled to the ground with a bone-shaking thud. The world spun. He groaned, pushing himself upright, brushing dust and twigs from his arms. Every nerve screamed caution. But there was no time to check for bruises or rest. He had to keep moving.

He broke into a run – eyes fixed on the road ahead – not realising what he'd left behind.

The pouch.

It had slipped from his satchel during the fall. Now it lay hidden among the fallen leaves, quiet and forgotten. Was it fate? A second warning, just as the first light had brought clarity, just as the bear had cast its shadow. Was something – or someone – trying to stop him? Zayd didn't know. He didn't look back. And the pouch, small and unremarkable, remained where it had fallen – waiting, buried in the hush of the forest floor.

VI

As the first stars began to pierce the velvet sky above Al-Waadi, Zayd finally stumbled into the palace courtyard. Exhausted, sore, and his thoughts in disarray. Across the stone floor, the Vizier paced like a storm gathering weight, his heavy steps slicing through the silence. The moment his gaze landed on Zayd, he surged forward like an arrow released from a taut bow – swift and direct.

In a heartbeat, he closed the distance between them, eyes scanning Zayd hungrily, searching for one thing. His fingers twitched at his side, eager to snatch the pouch the moment it appeared. More than three days had passed since Zayd had been sent on this errand. His absence had stretched into the realm of suspicion. A delay he could not explain away.

Unfamiliar paths, hostile terrain, and a string of misfortunes had turned a simple delivery into something far more harrowing. The toll of getting lost lingered in Zayd's weary movements, evident in the fatigue etched on his face. Though he had not yet realised the full extent of his misstep, the knowledge that he had failed to return within the Vizier's strict timeline loomed over him like a dark cloud.

"Where is it?" the Vizier demanded.

Zayd's heart pounded wildly. His hands dove into his satchel, rummaging through its contents with rising desperation. Panic tightened his chest as his fingers met only the coarse lining of an empty bag. He fumbled through his pockets – left, then right – coming up equally empty. A cold dread gripped him, rooting his feet to stone.

"It… it must've fallen," he stammered.

Of all moments to fail, why now? His true first error and it threatened not only the trust he had built over the years of quiet service, but his very place in the palace.

"I-I had to climb a tree, there was a bear – "

The Vizier raised a hand, silencing him with a look. His face darkened. Though Zayd braced for an outburst, the Vizier's voice dropped to a chilling whisper, far more menacing than a shout.

"So… you lost it."

Zayd opened his mouth, struggling to find an excuse, but the words died before they could form. Despite his short stature, the Vizier loomed over him, his presence suffocating, his glare pressing down like a physical weight.

"You fool!" His words dripped with fury.

"One task."

"I gave you one task."

"And somehow, you failed in a way that even I could not have anticipated. Tell me, Zayd, was the instruction too complex? Or is it simply that you cannot be trusted with matters of importance?"

Zayd's cheeks burned, shame washing over him.

"I – "

"You," the Vizier spat, cutting him off, "had the gall to return here empty-handed and expect forgiveness?" His eyes flashed with rage.

In a blur, his hand moved before Zayd could react – a sharp stinging slap across the face. The blow cracked through the courtyard. Zayd staggered back, clutching his cheek as pain bloomed like fire across his skin.

"Do you have any idea what you've cost me?"

Zayd fell to the ground, his knees scraping against the stone. The sting of failure coursing through him.

"Respected Vizier, please," he gasped, voice shaking. "I'll go back. I'll search every inch until I find it. Just give me – "

But the Vizier wasn't listening. He was already retreating into his own storm of calculation, assessing how much had been lost, and how quickly he might salvage his plan. This failure was not just an inconvenience – it threatened to unravel a wicked plot, years in the making. He couldn't afford this setback.

He had to act. Fast.

For Zayd, time seemed to stretch without end. Not in minutes or moments, but in dread, each breath steeped in uncertainty. How could he possibly extinguish the raging fire before him? How could he possibly reason with someone so consumed by rage?

"There will be no second chance." The Vizier's voice was ice.

"I always knew you were useless."

"Guards." The word rang out like a judgment. "Take him away. I'll decide later what to do with him. Let the dungeon remind him of what failure tastes like."

Two guards moved without question, their hands closing roughly around Zayd's arms as he struggled, fear overtaking his voice.

"Please! I'll fix this! Please – "

"Enough!" the Vizier barked, turning away in disgust.

The taste of failure was bitter. But even in the lowest moments, as he was being dragged away towards his punishment, something stirred in Zayd's mind. Perhaps a glimmer of hope amidst his despair. Was this really how all of this would end?

The people of Al-Waadi often said that a horse, left to its own pace, finds a truer path. That sometimes, loosening one's grip brings the destination nearer. Not every journey needs force. Some must simply be waited upon. In the same way, surrendering control might allow fate to weave a better course than any man could force. Just as a river carves its way through the land, shaping it over time, so too did fate flow through their lives, guiding each twist and turn, invisible yet undeniable.

To resist was futile.

There was wisdom, he realised, in yielding. In letting go of fear. In flowing with the current, rather than fighting against it. A strange calm settled over him and he stopped resisting. Maybe he wasn't being cast aside. Maybe he was being redirected. Perhaps – just perhaps – destiny was about to reveal itself in a way that required him to just sit back and observe. But then –

A splash!

Sharp and sudden, shattering the stillness of the courtyard. Everyone froze. Heads turned. Zayd held his breath. From the basin-pool at the centre of the courtyard, something stirred.

A figure rose – drenched, but his thin frame trembled with energy. His eyes aglow with a strange unearthly light. Water poured from his tunic as he stepped forward, and then he laughed. Not the laugh of madness, nor confidence, but something else. Something unsettling and bold. The sound echoed across the stones, rich with timing, as though it had been waiting for just this moment to emerge. And in that laugh, Zayd felt the balance of the world shift.

Fate, it seemed, had arrived…

Part II

Kneading Change

I

"I *did it!" the man cried, laughter spilling from his lips as* he took in the astonished faces surrounding him. "Across the skies – I truly flew!"

His laughter rang through the courtyard, wild and triumphant, alive with the thrill of defying death. He could hardly believe it himself. His flight, the fall, the survival. The sound carried an infectious energy, filling the air with a strange wonder, as if reality had momentarily shifted to make room for the impossible. Knee-deep in the courtyard pool, water streamed down his soaked tunic, clinging to a wiry frame shaped more by time than strength. Silver-streaked hair framed his face, his short grey beard, dripped. His warm brown eyes, lined with age, gleamed with exhilaration – an almost childlike wonder.

He barely registered the tension thick in the air. This was his moment. He had flown. After all, who wouldn't be captivated by that? Surely, that was reason enough to ignore the wary glances now fixed upon him. But perhaps not.

The Vizier was present, and the circumstances wouldn't allow for such indulgence. A guard took a cautious step forward, his eyes wide with disbelief as he stared at this man who had just fallen from the sky. The sight was so absurd, so unbelievable, that it left him questioning whether he was even real.

"Step out of the water." The guard commanded, trying to sound authoritative, but the fear in his eyes and the slight tremor of his hands betrayed his intimidating facade.

It was obvious that he was struggling to comprehend the absurdity of it all. It was one thing to confront a lunatic. It was quite another to do so when that lunatic had just fallen from the sky. It wasn't until the man caught sight of the guard's sword that the thrill of flight began to wane. His exhilaration faded as the stark reality of the courtyard closed in around him. The night sky, once vast and filled with wonder, now seemed darker, pressing down on him. His eyes swept across the tense gathering. First, they landed on the two guards, their armour glinting under the torchlight, hands hovering near their weapons.

But it was the young man off to the side that made him pause. And for the briefest moment, something passed between them – not recognition, but resonance. As though their fates had once brushed shoulders in a dream neither remembered. He stood apart, slumped with quiet despair. Not the posture of a traitor, nor a fool – but of someone on the verge of being broken. A man condemned before his time.

For the first time since his plunge from the sky, the man felt his own absurdity ebb. He was no longer just a wild dreamer crashing into the night. He had landed in the heart of something far greater than himself. With a hesitant step forward, he raised his hands, palms outward – a universal gesture of peace.

"Forgive me, esteemed sirs!" he declared, his voice an odd mix of excitement and nervousness.

"It seems I have rather unexpectedly landed in your midst!" He chuckled, a light-hearted sound that felt out of place in the tense atmosphere.

"What a curious turn of events! I had no intention of intruding upon such an important gathering. I assure you, my descent from the sky was entirely unplanned!" His eyes sparkled with the remnants of joy, even as he took in the serious faces around him.

"But here I am, and for that, I sincerely apologise." His gaze landed on the short, imposing figure of the Vizier, and a spark of recognition lit up his face. *Have I truly land-*

ed in the courtyard of the grand palace? he thought. A spark of disbelief crossed his mind, as he took in the three men before him, their stern expressions assessing him with quiet menace.

"Ah! The esteemed Vizier of Al-Waadi!" he exclaimed.

The kingdom knew him well; his appearance was familiar from parades and grand ceremonies where his presence commanded attention.

"I never expected to find myself so close to you, much less within palace walls!" He chuckled nervously, water still dripping from his beard.

"Forgive my unceremonious entrance, respected Vizier. I assure you; I meant no intrusion. It appears I've stumbled into something far more serious than I anticipated!"

"What a peculiar night it has been, wouldn't you agree?"

For a brief moment, the Vizier's fury wavered, giving way to bewilderment. His piercing gaze locked onto the drenched, dishevelled figure before him – an unexpected intruder who had quite literally fallen from the sky.

How? The question pounded in his mind. *How had this man survived such a fall? What twist of fate had delivered him, unharmed, into the heart of the palace? And, most unsettling of all – why was he so utterly... odd?*

The Vizier narrowed his eyes, the balance of the moment shifting. The night had begun with ominous purpose, yet now, it crackled with absurdity. He wrestled with his instincts, unsure whether to dismiss this man as a fool or recognise him as something more. A sign, a disruption, or perhaps even an opportunity. The Vizier shook off his bewilderment, regaining his composure as he focused on the peculiar man before him.

"Enough of this nonsense. Who are you?" He snapped, there was no room in him for softness.

"What are you doing here?"

"And how exactly, did you soar through the skies?" Each question pulled him further from his momentary confusion, grounding him in his usual sharpness.

He studied the man closely, his mind raced to piece together this extraordinary puzzle that had so unexpectedly invaded his world.

"Ah, yes… quite the entrance, I'll admit." The man muttered, glancing skyward as if considering another attempt.

"One doesn't fall from the clouds every day, I suppose."

He laughed – a deep, hearty laugh, rich with sincerity, but utterly misplaced given the seriousness of the moment. Then, as if flipping through the pages of his own mind, his expression shifted.

"But you see, esteemed Vizier, there is nothing in this world quite like flying!" His eyes sparkled with genuine awe, whilst his voice swelled with conviction, as though revealing some grand truth.

"It's a thrill no man should live without. Though the landing..." He paused, casting a sheepish glance at the basin he had crashed into.

"...Yes, that part needs work." He cleared his throat, noticing the Vizier's unamused glare but clearly too enraptured by his own achievement to stop.

"Ah, yes. You wouldn't believe it, truly, it's as if the sky takes you into its arms... but maybe that's a tale for another time." He gave a small bow.

"Forgive me, Vizier. I didn't exactly... plan to land here before you."

The Vizier's piercing eyes never left the strange man. This man – drenched, rambling, outlandish – had silenced the guards, derailed his night and somehow held the room. It wasn't often that anything could sway his mind from his purpose, least of all a ragged figure with a dripping beard and wild eyes. But here he was, forgetting even Zayd's presence, his sharp mind utterly captivated. This peculiar man who had fallen out of the heavens, unscathed and laughing, spoke of flying as if it were no more unusual than a walk through the marketplace. He scanned the man, searching for signs of deceit or trickery, for surely no ordinary person could do what this one claimed. Was he a madman? A sorcerer? A sign? The Vizier didn't know. But he wanted answers.

"Explain," the Vizier commanded.

"Every detail."

Even Zayd leaned forward, forgetting his own doom. The guards were motionless. All eyes fixed on this dripping, bewildering figure. He grinned – mischievous, almost reckless – as if savouring the chance to share a tale that defied the very laws of the world. He stepped forward. Lifted his hands.

"Ah, if you only knew where it began…" The memory itself sent a jolt of excitement through him.

"Gather close."

"For this tale may carry you further than you've ever dreamed." And with that – he began.

II

The man cleared his throat dramatically, his eyes glancing around the courtyard as if to make sure he had everyone's undivided attention.

"Ah, where to begin... Where to begin?" he mused, rubbing his chin, his tone rich with giddy anticipation, like a man about to unveil a great secret.

"My name is Hassan, a baker." He paused, letting the words settle before adding, with unmistakable pride. "Yes, that's right – a simple baker. I make the best bread in all of Al-Waadi." He scanned over the audience, searching for a hint of recognition, perhaps expecting murmurs of agreement. Surely, someone had heard of his legendary loaves? After all, according to Hassan it was the best bread in all of Al-Waadi. But the faces staring back at him remained impassive. Hassan's proud smile faltered just a touch, but he pressed on, undeterred.

"No, really," he insisted, "it is the best bread in Al-Waadi."

"Now, let me tell you, friends. Though I've lived as a humble baker, I've often wondered if this was truly the path the Almighty had set for me. A simple life, yes. A roof over my head, a family at my side, and dough that, on most days, rose as it should. A man could live well on such things. And I was content. Or at least, I told myself I was.

"But you see, I was a man of many passions. Oh yes, more than you might think. As a young man, my mind wandered far beyond my bakery walls. Poetry, stargazing, even dabbling with odd contraptions, though most of my inventions barely held together about as well as a poorly kneaded loaf. There was a time I thought I'd travel to distant lands, see strange sights, explore secrets beyond my little corner of Al-Waadi. I could have been many things, perhaps.

"But, love... now, there's a tricksy thing, isn't it? There I was, full of dreams and fancies – like most foolish young men – thinking I'd see the world, maybe even become someone grand. But then, wouldn't you know it? Along came love, wearing a smile so warm it could melt stone. And in an instant, my grand plans faded like smoke in the desert wind. I surrendered to it. Gave my heart willingly to the woman who had claimed it without even trying.

"And, well, with love came marriage. I thought, *Here's my life now – a simple, honest one.* And what better way to build a future than turning my hands to bread? I told myself I'd make a proper life for my family. Something solid, unshakeable. And I thought, there's always demand for bread, isn't there? So, I poured all my ambition into that bakery, kneading my dreams into every loaf. Each loaf, I told myself, was like a stone in the sturdy house I was building for them. I thought it was noble, you see, to create something they could rely on. But I never left time for the rest of me. The part that once wanted to see strange lands, marvel at the stars, craft new things with my hands. And as the years went by, well... I found myself trapped within the very walls I'd built. Four walls and a bakery – a cage of my own making. Slowly, my youth slipped through my fingers like grains of flour, scattering before I could grasp them.

"My ambitions? They sat untouched, gathering dust like a forgotten compass tucked away on a high shelf, left to sit rather than guide me forward. A part of me blamed love, I'll admit. A little voice whispered, *had I not fallen in love, I'd have been someone else. I might have had the life I once dreamed of.*

"I knew it was a wretched thought, so I buried it deep, never spoke it aloud – not to a soul. But a buried seed still grows and that little seed of resentment took root in my heart. So, one day, I raised my hands up to the Almighty, and I prayed, not for riches, not for escape, but to be rid of that bitterness. I asked for my heart to be scrubbed clean of those selfish thoughts. And you know... as I stood there, hands lifted, it struck me. A thought like a lightning bolt.

"Maybe it was me.

"It wasn't that I had fallen in love. Truly, some of the most joyous moments of my life have been spent with my wife. No, it wasn't her, or even the family I had built. But I realised that while I'd been blaming life for what it had not given me, I'd been the one sitting in my bakery, day after day, kneading the same dough. What was stopping me from fulfilling my ambitions?

"The answer wasn't in the bread. It wasn't in the bakery or in the steady routine I had convinced myself was enough. No, the answer was in me. I had been too afraid to step out. Too comfortable to reach for something greater. Too scared to live anything other than a quiet, predictable life. But deep down, I knew something had to change. I had spent so many years telling myself I was building a stable life, but I hadn't built anything. I'd built a cage. A cage of comfort and fear.

"Perhaps because I'd convinced myself that I was waiting for fate to knock on my door, that one day, it would hand me the keys to something greater. But the more I thought about it, the more I realised: life doesn't just hand you anything. You have to chase it. Fate is something you make, not something you wait for.

"*The Almighty doesn't change the condition of a man until the man changes what's within himself, does He?*

"You see, these thoughts gave me hope. That perhaps I could still do something with my life – bring some excitement into it. No matter how many layers of darkness surround you, as long as the spark of hope remains, it can be ignited to light up your life. That spark, it had flared to life inside me at last.

"I could feel it. I was going to make a change. I didn't know how, just yet, or what exactly I'd be leaping into, but I knew one thing for certain: I had spent enough time dreaming.

"It was time to live."

III

"So, there I was. It was supposed to be just another day, like any other. The sun rose, the bakery filled with that familiar warmth, and I went about my work as usual, muttering and rambling on to myself about this and that. And there she was, calm as anything, sorting the flour, completely oblivious to the wild ideas brewing inside me.

"I had been thinking of ways that I could satiate this desire for freedom, a yearning that had been building now for some time. I longed for something – anything – that might break the monotony of life within the four walls of the bakery. Perhaps foolishly, I blurted this out to my wife that day. The words came rushing out, without thought or caution, as though I could somehow just toss this great burden of uncertainty into the air and hope it would land neatly somewhere.

"It was foolish because I hadn't prepared myself for the depth of what I was saying, nor for how she might react. I hadn't fully processed what I was feeling, but here I was, testing the waters of my dissatisfaction with just a casual remark. I had no idea how she would respond to hearing such a deep, unspoken part of myself.

" 'Tell me,' I said, as casually as one might ask about the weather. 'Do you ever wonder if fate is waiting for us to make the first move?

" 'That maybe, we've got to meet it halfway instead of standing here, waiting for life to just happen to us?'

"She gave me that look – the one that said, *here he goes again with his nonsense.* But by then, I was too far gone. The words had a life of their own, and I couldn't stop them now.

" 'I want to feel free,' I told her.

She raised an eyebrow, clearly puzzled. 'What are you talking about now, Hassan?'

"But I pressed on, my thoughts spilling out faster than I could catch them. It wasn't so much that I was speaking to her. It was more that I was trying to speak to myself. I was seeking validation for the words I was finally giving life to, looking for someone to confirm that maybe, just maybe, there was something more to all this than a simple craving for excitement. That there was something more waiting beyond the life I had settled into. However, that statement seemed to disturb her.

" 'Free?' She asked. 'Do you feel caged by me, then?'

"She had turned my words inwards, misunderstanding my meaning, but I was too deep in my own thoughts to correct her.

"I pressed on. 'Every day, I look up at the birds soaring freely in the sky, while I feel stuck here, confined within the same four walls. It's as though they are mocking me – gliding effortlessly through the air while I am anchored to the ground.'

"She sighed. 'Where is this coming from now?' You have a family that loves you, a stable life, what more could you want?'

" 'Why do you always find something to complain about?'

"Ah, how she misunderstood, again. It wasn't that I was ungrateful for what I had – far from it. I loved my family more than anything, and yes, I had stability. But I couldn't shake the feeling that I had built a box around myself. I had what many would consider enough. A family, a home, love, security.

"But why stop there? Why should those things mean I had to stop trying to add to my life? Why should achieving them mean settling down into a life of endless repetition? Why not take the next step and enrich it with something new, something exciting? To expand, to explore, to enrich what I already had?

"I wasn't trying to escape what I had. I wanted to live alongside it, *more* than it. I had the foundation, now why not build something that stirred the heart?

" 'Why can't I be like the birds?' I almost shouted.

" 'I too can soar; I too can find purpose beyond this.'

"But that's when it happened – she chuckled. Chuckled, as if my yearning for something greater – for a life that reached beyond the everyday – was nothing more than a passing whim. Perhaps I misunderstood that chuckle. Maybe she wasn't mocking me at all. People often laughed at my thoughts, and I suppose they were amusing now and then. But I was being serious. This time, I needed her to understand. I needed comfort, not a laugh. But to her, it was just another one of my wild thoughts.

" 'Hassan, you're talking nonsense,' she said, shaking her head with a smile.

" 'You've got a good life here. Stop dreaming about things that can never be.'

"Her words stung more than I cared to admit. She misunderstood me. To her, my words were just complaints. A sign that I'd grown ungrateful. Restless for no reason at all. It wasn't nonsense. I wanted to tell her, but the words wouldn't come. Instead, something else took root inside me, like a ship's sail catching the first pull of the wind.

" 'It's not nonsense, I tell you,' I muttered under my breath, my resolve building.

" 'Watch me. I too will fly.'

"For her, this was just another argument. She turned, muttering something about me and my 'dreams,' and left the bakery, her frustration clear in her steps. But as the door closed behind her... Something inside me solidified. I wasn't going to stay in this place, stuck in this small life, baking the same loaves day after day.

"No.

"I was going to prove her wrong. I was going to prove to her – and to myself – that I could be more. I wasn't going to wait for fate to hand me anything. I was going to make my own fate.

"And by the time I returned, I'd show her –

"I'd show everyone –

"That was the moment everything changed."

IV

"I rose the next morning, just before dawn, when the world's still soft and quiet. And instead of making my way towards the bakery, I turned in the other direction – out towards

the hills, into the open air, into the unknown. For the first time in years, I didn't even glance at the bakery; it had no hold on me that morning. I had my heart set on something... more. I didn't know yet what that more was, but I knew it was waiting for me somewhere beyond the usual walls. As I walked, I felt a strange thrill rising in me, like I was tasting freedom for the first time in years. There's a promise in the air at dawn, as if the world is reminding us that each morning holds a new start, a chance to choose again. It was as if the earth itself was whispering to me: *come, today's a blank page – what will you make of it?*

"And that morning, I wanted to write something entirely different. Why should each day be nothing more than a copy of the last? It dawned on me that we may often lock ourselves into our own lives, sticking to what's safe, what's familiar. We tie ourselves to routine, our duties, as if duty and repetition are all we were made for. But what if each sunrise was an invitation to step beyond that?

"What if, instead of confining ourselves to a life of repetition, we reached for a life that made our hearts race, that breathed new purpose into our days?

"There's so much more to a man than his habits, so much more to a day than just surviving it. And so, I kept walking. That morning, I felt like a child taking his first steps beyond familiar walls, eyes wide with wonder, reaching out to touch a world he's only dreamed of.

"Now, mind you, I hadn't the faintest clue where I was headed. But that didn't matter. I just needed to feel something stirring in me again. I thought, *maybe I'd find an adventure, something to shake off the dust and make me feel alive. You know…make up for all those years I'd been standing still.*

"But as I'm wandering around with my grand thoughts of freedom, her words clung to me like a shadow. I kept seeing her face, hearing her chuckle, as if my longing for something bigger than daily routine was just some joke. I thought I could shake it off, ignore her voice in my head, but… there she was, laughing at me with every step I took. Then…then it hit me.

"A challenge, clear as the morning light! If she thought my dreams of soaring were so silly, then I'd do the one thing no one would ever expect from a baker who'd never so much as left the city…

"No more metaphors. If I was going to dream, I'd dream loud enough for the whole world to hear it. I would fly. Not in some lofty, poetic sense – no!

"I mean I would *literally* fly.

"And so, I spent that whole first day scouring the city, hunting for anything remotely useful – bits of wood, old cloth, even some wax. I searched through courtyards, peered into workshops, and rummaged through store-rooms, gathering every strange scrap like a man possessed. In my mind, though, it was all part of a grand plan. The more I found, the clearer it became. The design, the wings, the way it would all come together. After that first day of gathering, I laid everything out before me: wood, cloth, leather bindings. I got to work crafting, shaping each piece with care, rekindling that old love for invention that I'd long buried beneath routine. Over several days, those scraps became something real.

"I cut the wood and stretched the fabric over each wing like a blacksmith shaping iron, bending and moulding each piece with purpose, until it took the form I had envisioned. Each step adding form to what had been just a wild thought. I worked until my hands were stiff, binding each piece with leather, sealing the seams with wax. There were a few mishaps – one or two unfortunate tumbles that sent my work table crashing – but nothing could stop me now.

"Finally, after days of sweat and tinkering, I took a step back. Before me lay the wings, gleaming in the morning light. Every piece in place, ready. It was as if all those scattered scraps had taken flight themselves, gathering into a creation more magnificent than I'd dared to imagine.

"I thought to myself, *this is it, Hassan. You've built your wings – now it's time to fly.*

"*Just picture it. Me, soaring above, proving her wrong!*

"These weren't just bits of cloth and wood anymore; they were the wings of a dreamer. And by heaven, I was going to soar.

"I strapped them to my arms ever so proud. In my mind, these were the wings of an eagle, powerful enough to lift me above everything I'd ever known. This was real. And now, all I needed was the right place to take flight. My eyes fell on the mountain outside the city of Al-Waadi. Tall and proud, it rose like a silent guardian, watching over Al-Waadi.

"It would be perfect.

"I'd climb to its peak by dawn, and from there, I'd launch myself into the sky, gliding right over the city for everyone to see. With one last look at my creation, I turned towards the mountain, ready to make my mark."

V

"*I made it up the mountain and I now stood at the edge, looking* down over the vast stretch of land below me. The wind was fierce, tugging at my makeshift wings, which felt like they might snap any second.

"Was I mad? Most certainly.

"Was all this necessary? Maybe not.

"But at that moment, none of that seemed to matter. I felt something I hadn't in years. A wild, uncontrollable surge of excitement. A belief that this was it. The moment when I would finally prove to myself that I could break free from the chains I'd wrapped around my own life. I looked down at the city of Al-Waadi, small and quiet below, oblivious to the fact that I was about to do something utterly ridiculous.

"Could I really fly?

"Was it just the fevered imaginings of a man who had spent too much time alone, crafting wings from wood and cloth like a fool?

"Maybe.

"But wasn't that what life was all about? Taking a step when no one else would. Believing in something, even if the world laughed? The wind howled, and I couldn't help but smile. I was shaking, but not from fear. No – I trembled with the thought of what this moment could mean. What if I did it? What if these wings, these ridiculous, lopsided things, actually worked? I could fly. I could soar over Al-Waadi, like the birds I envied. Like I imagined I would. Escaping the pull of routine that had held me down for so long. And yet...

"As the wind ruffled through the makeshift wings, I had to ask myself: Was this really about freedom? Or was I just running away from something? A life I built. A family I loved. A business that fed me. Was this truly the answer to everything? Or was it just my way of avoiding the quiet truth that maybe…

"I just wanted to matter beyond the bakery, beyond the walls I had boxed myself into. My heart pounded against my ribs. But I couldn't turn back now. There was no time for hesitation. The world was waiting. And I wasn't about to spend another moment in that same dusty shop, forever wondering, *what if?*

"So, with a grin – perhaps one a little wilder than I intended – I spread my arms wide, feeling the wind catch the edges of my wings, and I announced aloud:

" 'Well, if I'm going to fall, let it be so free they mistake it for flight.'

"And with that, I jumped…

"As I leapt into the air, there was a moment, just a breath, where time seemed to stretch and bend. The world blurred around me, and I closed my eyes. For a second, it was as if I was floating in the void. Not quite falling, not yet soaring. Just suspended between the two. A stillness that made everything else fade away. The wind, the ground, even the thundering of my heart. There was just silence. As if the world was holding its breath for me. The darkness behind my closed eyelids felt vast and endless, like the very sky itself was swallowing me whole. For that one heartbeat, I belonged to the air. Then, the world came rushing back.

"Would this moment be the one where I finally understood something greater? Or would it remain as nothing but a fleeting thought, swallowed by the unknown? I couldn't tell. Maybe it would always be darkness, this split-second of uncertainty – never knowing whether I was about to rise or fall. Or maybe, just maybe, when I opened my eyes, there would be light. A flash of brilliance. A spark that would prove all this madness had a purpose.

"I didn't know. But I had to find out.

"So, I opened my eyes.

"I immediately wished I hadn't...

"It felt safer with my eyes closed, as if I could hold on to the freedom of the moment just a little longer. What I saw wasn't the grand sky of freedom I'd imagined, nor was it the majestic flight of some hero from the stories. No – what I saw was the ground hurtling towards me with an alarming speed. And the very real possibility that I was about to meet it in a way that would leave me wishing for a bit more time to reconsider my life choices.

" 'Okay, Hassan,' I muttered to myself.

" 'This may have been a mistake. A *huge* mistake.'

The ground was getting closer, much closer. I flailed my arms, hoping the wings – these pitiful excuses for wings – might actually work. But they didn't. They flapped uselessly in the wind, like a bird who had just realised it forgot how to fly. Instead, the wind slapped me sideways like a leather strap across the face, sending me spinning in a way that I'm fairly certain was not part of my original flight plan.

" 'Oh, come on!' I shouted at the sky, because what else was I going to blame?

" 'Is this really how my story ends? Wings and wax and regret?'

"And yet…

"Somewhere in the wild flailing, in the chaos of feathers and fear – I laughed. It wasn't a heroic laugh. It was the desperate, borderline, manic chuckle of a man realising he may have very literally flown too close to the sun –

"Or at least, too far from common sense.

"But even as the earth came roaring closer, one thought stayed firm in my mind, louder than all the noise: *At least I tried.*

" 'Focus!' I told myself, though I wasn't sure what I was supposed to focus on anymore.

" 'Remember your dreams! You're a man of destiny! The world is yours!'

"And then –

"Wait a minute. I felt it. A shift. A pull. For a brief, miraculous second, the wind caught beneath my wings. My body jolted. My stomach flipped. I wasn't falling. Was I… floating? A strange, exhilarating burst of joy shot through me.

"*I was flying!*

"All panic evaporated. I wasn't plummeting, I wasn't tumbling. The wind was under my wings, my feet off the ground. I wasn't soaring – not quite –

"But I was... gliding.

"I hadn't expected it to feel like this, I hadn't imagined the way the air would carry me, but there I was, in the sky with the city of Al-Waadi laid out beneath me.

" 'Ha!' I shouted, grinning like a fool.

" 'I'm actually doing it! I'm – '

"And then…

"Just as quickly, the joy turned to terror. My heart skipped a beat. A thought struck me: *How in the name of the heavens am I going to land?* I hadn't exactly planned for the part where I'd need to touch the ground again. All that talk about freedom and destiny came crashing down into one blinding truth: *What on earth was I doing?*

"The thought hit me so hard, I forgot how to fly alto-gether. Panic surged. My limbs flailed. Before I knew it, I was nosediving through the air again, arms and wings thrashing wildly, as if I could outrun the terror. The wind slapped against my face, each gust more frantic than the last, as though it too was mocking me for my foolishness. I had never thought this part through. Sure, I had the wings – oh yes, I'd built them myself: every splinter of wood, every scrap of cloth. I'd imagined the soaring, the freedom, the glory. But did I – Hassan the baker – think about what came after the leap?

"No.

"And that, my friends, was my flaw. I was so caught up in the thrill of it all, so driven by the desire to feel alive and free, to taste something more than the rise and fall of dough, that I forgot to ask the most important question of all:

"*What comes next?*

"I hadn't planned for the descent, the landing, or even the possibility that I might need to control this chaotic flight. Life, it turns out, is a lot like this. We may chase our dreams with hearts on fire. We may rush headlong into the unknown, thinking that the wind will always carry us, that the wings will hold us up. But we forget – oh, how we forget – the flight is only half the story.

"It's the landing that defines us. It's that sharp, sobering moment when the soaring ends, and we're left scrambling to figure out how to stand on our own two feet once more. For a few glorious seconds, I soared. Well... glided. But come on – let me have my moment. It felt amazing. Like I was finally doing something that mattered, something that had weight beyond bread and baking. But as the ground rushed up to meet me once more, that strange, fluttering joy in my chest was replaced with a sharp, gut-clenching panic. I was falling. Truly, absolutely, uncontrollably falling.

"I flapped my arms.

"What in the world was I doing? The wings were fluttering around like the flag in a storm, and I had no idea how to stop or steer. Should I have pulled them in? Should I have tried to dive? I had no idea –

"I hadn't thought it through. It wasn't enough to just leap. It never is. It wasn't enough to throw yourself into the world with no sense of what's ahead. No matter how bold, how beautiful –

"It means little if you haven't thought about where you'll land. You have to think beyond the moment and consider what's to come. You have to live with intention, not just impulse. You need to be ready for the fall as much as for the flight. And so, there I was, mid-air.

"My wings useless. My future uncertain. And for the first time in this journey, I thought:

"Maybe I should have stayed in the bakery."

VI

"Time had slowed to a crawl. A near standstill. Everything moved strangely – like the world had paused, just for me. I hung there in the air, dangling between life and a very sudden death. I was still falling, of course – my poor excuse for wings dancing helplessly in the air – but in that instant, it no longer felt like I was caught between the sky and the ground. I was suspended between who I had been… and who I might have become.

"And then, like a lantern flickering to life in the dark, the memories came. I saw her. Not in the grand gestures, but in the quiet, steady ones. The way she stood by me when the days were harder than I'd ever admit. When the strain of the world felt too much to bear, she was there, always there. Her hands steady, her voice a calm reminder that I could carry on.

"She'd never say much, but she didn't need to. She had a way of simply holding things together with a quiet strength I never quite knew how to repay. I remembered the way she cared for our children. How, even after the longest days, she greeted them with a smile that reached her eyes. How many times had I come home exhausted, only to find her waiting, light in her eyes, arms open, heart full? Her love was patient. Unshaken. Fierce in its gentleness. No matter how little I had to offer, she gave more than I could ever deserve.

"And I remembered the hard moments too. The arguments, the silences, the sharp words that sometimes spilled when we didn't know where else to put our fear. But even in those moments, she fought for us. Even when I couldn't see the same things she did. Even in every misunderstanding, every disagreement, every moment when we were at odds, I knew, deep down, that her passion was just her way of wanting the best for us. Believing in me, even when I couldn't see it myself.

"That was what love was.

"Not the grand declarations or sweeping gestures. Not the kind you write poems about, though perhaps it deserved one.

"No.

"It was quieter than that. Stronger. It was the kind of love you find in forgiveness given before it's even asked for. In the courage to endure when it would be easier to walk. In a heart that beats not just for itself, but for others.

"She never asked for more than I could give, though she deserved the world. Just as clearly as I saw her love, the thoughts that had driven me to leap in the first place crept back in. Persistent, sharp and impossible to ignore. Had I settled too soon? Had I reached far enough? Had I mistaken routine for purpose? Was this… this mad, reckless leap, the sum of my life? One brief act of escape before…

"…Nothing?

"It was strange. The thought of falling terrified me. But what scared me more – far more – was that this was my end. I had spent my days half-living. Safe and predictable. Never fully offering myself to the world. Had I lived at all? I closed my eyes. I thought my story was just beginning, but this was to be the end. I prayed. Not for a miracle. Just for a chance. *Let this madness not be the end. Let me live. Let me learn.*

"It was odd. How vivid every thought became in that single, drawn-out heartbeat. Even now, I remember everything. I prayed for…

"*One more day...*

"To see that routine was never the enemy – only my forgetting. That life isn't found beyond the ordinary, but within it. And with intention, even the smallest act can become a prayer, a purpose, a beginning.

"One more hour...

"To notice the love already around me – soft, quiet, waiting to be seen. To let go of the small things that kept hearts apart.

"To say what should've been said. To forgive.

"To meet each other in the space between pride and tenderness. For in the end, life is measured not by what we held onto, but by what we chose to set free.

"One more moment...

"To realise this is it.

"Not the life we chase, but the one already unfolding in front of us. Not something distant, but present. A breath. A choice. A quiet chance to live like we mean it.

"And maybe that's what I was chasing all along. Not escape. But a reason to wake up again. To feel the life I already had as if for the first time.

"And then, as if summoned by the desperation of my prayers, something shifted. A nudge in the air, or maybe it was my own instinctive flapping finding form. My body angled, not in a free fall anymore – not exactly. My eyes shot open. And somehow…

"I was gliding again. Not gracefully. Not heroically. But steering. Just enough. Just enough to avoid an untimely impact with the rocks below. And by some miracle, I found myself drifting towards the forest of Al-Waadi. The trees drew closer. I could see every leaf, every branch, every scratch waiting to catch me. I braced myself. And sure enough, the trees did what I hoped they would do. They broke my fall, with a flurry of snapping limbs, a symphony of scratching bark and startled birds. I had landed in a tangled heap. Undignified. Winded. Bruised. But most important of all, alive.

VII

"For a long moment, I just lay there, tangled in branches, blinking, staring up at the sky as if the heavens themselves might lean down and tell me what had just happened. Was I dead? If so, death had a lot more splinters than I'd been led to believe. Cautiously, I tried to sit up, wincing as every inch of me seemed to groan in protest. I pinched myself, once, then again, just to make sure.

"Yes, I was alive.

"The truth hit me all at once, and I let out a cheer so loud that birds scattered from the trees. I'd done it!

"Well, *sort* of done it. I'd leapt from the mountain, twisted wildly through the sky, and, somehow, managed to land in one piece. If there'd been a crowd, I'd have taken a bow right there on the forest floor. I scrambled to my feet, half-limping, half-laughing, looking around at the wreckage of my 'wings' – if you could even call them that anymore. Bits of wood and torn cloth were scattered around, like the wreckage of a kite that had aimed far too high.

" 'Well,' I muttered, gathering up the remains. 'I suppose every great invention looks a bit rough at first...'

"The thrill still buzzed through my bones, and I couldn't wipe the grin off my face. Yes, it had been terrifying. Yes, I'd spun about like a madman and forgotten about landing. And, yes, I had prayed harder than I ever had in my life. But still – I *had flown*!

"Or, at least... *almost.* In my mind, I was practically soaring with the eagles. I looked around, scratching my head at the ruins. All those thoughts... that whole *grand revelation.* I'd seen my life flash before my eyes, hadn't I? I'd promised to cherish every breath, every hour, every *single moment* with the people I loved. So, the *sensible* thing – the truly wise thing – would be to tuck this whole idea away forever. Wouldn't it?

"I chuckled at the thought.

"But the memory of that leap...

"The thrill as the ground dropped away, the wind swept beneath the wings, and the sky seemed to open just for me – my body still surged with the wild rush. I'd never felt anything like it in my life. From now on, I was a baker by name and a flier by… well, maybe, let me not get ahead of myself. So far, it had only been one morning, but what a morning it was. It was glorious. And yes, alright, it *had* been mad. Borderline disastrous, even. But what a *story* it would've been… *if* someone had actually seen it.

"Aha!

"That was the trouble. I realised, no one had seen it. Not a single soul. I could go back to the city and tell them the whole tale, but who'd believe me?

" 'Hassan? Flying?' They'd laugh.

" 'The man who can barely keep his balance on solid ground?'

"Or worse, they'd think it was a joke gone too far, a tale spun to pass the time at the tea house.

"No.

"It didn't feel right. It felt, in fact, unfinished. A half-dream, half-baked and left to cool on the counter, unappreciated and unseen.

" 'Alright.' I muttered, as if arguing with myself.

" 'Yes, I almost died. Yes, my heart is still hammering. And no, I probably shouldn't tempt fate.'

"I looked at the splintered wings in my hands.

" 'But who's to say that fate didn't *intend* for me to make it out alright?'

" 'And besides…' I chuckled to myself, lifting the broken frame.

" '…When will I ever have a chance like this again?'

"A man doesn't get to live on the edge every day.

"It dawned on me just then – was this mad venture so different from life itself? We wake, we rise, we step into each day not knowing how we'll land by dusk. I'd always played it safe in the bakery. Making just enough bread, just enough money, and a neat little name for myself. But maybe life needed a few big leaps. A few risks that bring us back to the very edge of everything we think we know. So, clutching those shredded wings, I smiled to myself. I'd mend them. Make them stronger. Set my sights even higher. Because the world was out there – waiting for mad dreamers like me. Now, let me tell you this…

"As I dusted myself off, brushed the leaves from my hair and picked twigs out from my clothes, something caught my eye. Nestled between the branches was a small, brown pouch. My heart skipped.

"We all know, according to tradition – if something's left unattended, well, it's fair game, isn't it? I picked it up. It was leather, worn, but solid, like it had been carried through countless journeys. I brushed off the leaves and turned it in my hand, smiling. Well, look at that. This could be the start of something. I stared at it, thinking of everything I'd just been through. Surely this was a sign. Proof that the universe had my back. After all, what were the chances? I leap into chaos, and find treasure waiting. I held it up as if to the sky. To the trees. To anyone that might have been watching. See?

"This is what you get for living boldly, for taking action, for doing something that others might call mad. This pouch, whatever it held, was my reward for daring to break free from my ordinary life. I could already see it – walking back into the house, showing my wife the pouch.

" 'Look,' I'd say. 'This came to me because I moved, because I acted, because I took a chance!'

"She would *have* to see it that way. It would show her that maybe there was something more to all this than the daily grind of the bakery. Maybe, just maybe, this crazy, foolish act wasn't all for nothing. Then again...

"I hadn't even opened it yet. Could be anything. A few coins. Some pebbles. Or worse – nothing at all. Still, the thrill bubbling inside me made it feel far more significant than it probably was. Either way, whatever was inside, I'd make it work. Because this pouch was proof that I'd done something today.

"Now…

As for how I was going to explain it all to my wife? Well. That was going to be another story.

VIII

The room had fallen into a strange stillness as Hassan's words hung in the air. His story had been so vividly told that, for a moment, the entire assembly had forgotten the present – lost in the madness of his flight, the thrill of his reckless adventure. The Vizier, his usual stern composure nowhere to be found, leaned forward like a child listening to a fantastical tale. His eyes gleamed, wide with wonder. Even the guards, usually statues of discipline, seemed to have softened. They hung on every word, as though they too were perched on the edge of a cliff, waiting to see whether Hassan would fly or fall. Then, the mention of the pouch. It was as though a bucket of cold water had been thrown over them all. The spell shattered.

Reality snapped back into place.

In an instant, the Vizier's expression twisted from rapt awe to disbelief. He straightened as the absurdity of the situation finally settled in. The calm, dreamy expression that had softened his features hardened once more into the cold, calculating gaze of a man who did not take kindly to surprises. Zayd sprang to his feet. His eyes blazed with a mix of triumph and urgency.

"You see, respected Vizier," he said, with a sharp and confident voice.

"I was telling the truth. That pouch – the one Hassan found – it must be the same one I lost when I fell from the tree."

Hassan blinked, not entirely understanding the importance of what Zayd was saying. But the Vizier? He inhaled deeply, steadying himself, but his soul rattled the bars of his chest, restless and riled. His once carefully laid plan was unravelling thread by thread. It was becoming painfully clear: everyone involved seemed either mad or hopelessly incompetent. The pouch – his pouch – wasn't lost after all, but had somehow found its way into the hands of this eccentric, wildly unpredictable man… right here in Al-Waadi. The sheer absurdity of it all nearly made his head spin. Yet, there was a glimmer of hope. If he could understand the situation fully. If he could dig through the layers of chaos and confusion, and understand what Hassan had done with the pouch, he might still salvage what remained of his intentions. He just needed to think.

Properly this time.

"Well then," he said with a clipped breath, "finish your tale."

He sounded impatient, but there was something else in his voice. A quiet fascination, perhaps. Despite every effort to remain detached, he couldn't help himself being drawn in. Hassan's tale was too strange, too unexpected. No matter how much he tried to convince himself otherwise, he just had to hear how this absurd story had brought this man crashing – quite literally – before him. Hassan hadn't given the pouch much thought. It was, after all, just another thing he'd stumbled across in the chaos of his day.

But a small suspicion stirred within him. A whisper at the back of his mind: What's going on here? What secrecy does that pouch hold? Zayd's urgency. That sharp interruption. The pouch was more important than Hassan had first realised. He shook off the thought, tucking it away in the far corner of his mind. Trying to regain his composure, Hassan fumbled for his words, stammering briefly. But after a brief hesitation, his rhythm found him once more. The story began to flow again, each word painting vivid images –

pulling the crowd back into its spell, once more, leaving everyone utterly engrossed.

"I burst through the door of my home, throwing it open with so much force it bounced off the wall, and straight into my face. Stunned for only a moment, I shook it off and barrelled forward, the excitement still surging through me. I flung the words into the room, unable to hold them back.

" 'I did it!'

"Of course…

"I was met with nothing but a startled silence. Perhaps she hadn't heard me. I said again, a little louder this time, a little more breathless.

'" I did it.'

" 'Did what, Hassan?' she asked, her tone flat, half-distracted, half-exasperated.

"She didn't even look up. Still weaving, still threading her needle through some delicate pattern as though I'd simply announced the neighbour's goat wandering in again. But I had to tell her. I had to share it.

" 'I flew!' I grinned, like a fool.

" 'Took to the skies, you hear me? Soared through the air like a bird – free as the wind! You should've seen it, my heart was – '

" 'You did what?' She set her work aside and finally looked up.

"Her expression was halfway between confusion and caution, like she was deciding whether this was nonsense to ignore or madness worth getting angry about. I felt the excitement leave me slowly, like steam rising from a cooling pot.

" 'I flew, I tell you!' I insisted, louder now – as if volume would lend the words credibility.

"Though, as I said it, I heard how ridiculous it sounded. But still, I pressed on.

" 'I crafted wings with my own two hands. Real wings! Not some child's toy. I leapt from the mountain. You should've seen it; anyone watching would've thought I was a falcon!'

"Her gaze sharpened, and I could feel it – this slow burn of disbelief creeping in. The silence between us stretched longer than I liked, and I watched her closely, my heart pounding in my ears, hoping, just hoping she would see it. The truth of what I had done, the exhilaration of it all. But no. Her lips pressed tight. The anger in her eyes became apparent. She folded her arms, pacing slowly towards me.

" 'Are you completely out of your mind, Hassan?'

" 'You said you jumped off a mountain?'

"I tried to answer. The words spilled out of me, eager to explain.

" 'I've never felt so alive; it was incredible! For just one moment, I – '

"She threw her hands up, silencing me.

" 'Alive?!'

" 'Is that what you call it? Risking your life? What if something happened to you?

" 'What if you – '

"She didn't finish. She didn't have to. The unspoken 'died' hung in the air like a heavy stone between us. I opened my mouth to argue, but she wasn't done. Her eyes caught the pouch I had tied so carefully to my tunic. She strode forward, snatched it from my side, fingers clenched around the leather.

" 'What's this? You risk your life and come back with this?'

"With a swift flick, she hurled it across the room. It hit the wall. Dropped. Lay still. *Well…That didn't go quite how I imagined.* I should've expected it. I suppose I deserved it. After all, there I was – full of excitement – while she was undoubtedly picturing how she'd have to pick up the pieces of our life if things had gone wrong. If I'd fallen. If I'd broken something. If I'd died.

"But…

"I just couldn't **shake** that feeling. I had lived. Truly lived. And no matter how foolish it seemed, I needed someone – anyone – to see that. To understand. I wasn't just a baker with foolish dreams. I had taken flight.

"I had done something.

"I stood there, staring at the pouch where it lay on the floor, hoping it would somehow vindicate the madness. Make it worthwhile. But she wasn't impressed. And honestly? I wasn't sure what I was trying to prove anymore. Maybe she was right. Maybe I was a fool for thinking that my madness would change anything.

" 'I guess you're right,' I said, turning away.

" 'I was foolish. But you know what? For once…'

'" I didn't feel like I was just going through the motions of life. I didn't feel like I was dragging myself through days I couldn't name. I felt – '

"I paused, searching for the right words to make her understand.

" 'I felt like I had lived.'

"She said nothing. Of course she didn't. I stood there for a long while. Thinking. Maybe I'd go back to the bakery. Give it up. Forget the whole mad idea. But what if I tried again? By heaven, even now, just remembering, the rush of wind, the open sky beneath me, the pulse of that perfect, untamed moment –

"My heart raced. What if I could really soar? Not for glory. Not for the story. Just to feel it. One more time. For now, I knew one thing: I'd never forget the way it felt to be alive.

"You see the beauty of a soft heart is that it lets in life's terrific emotions; love, serenity, gratitude, just some of the beautiful feelings that enter the soul through the gateway of the heart. A heart like that is open, vulnerable, waiting for inspiration to pass through it and stir up powerful emotions, the kind that make you feel you can uproot a tree or overturn a mountain. But a hardened heart? It shuts out those emotions, barring the way and growing colder with each passing year. And so, maybe it's no surprise I ended up here. I've always tried to keep my heart open – not to chaos, but to meaning. To let wonder in, to let passion breathe. A soft heart doesn't chase every wild whim. It listens. It feels deeply. It knows when something matters.

"That's why, even in the face of fear, of her concern, her anger, something in me still stirred. Not in defiance of her love, but in honour of the life we're meant to live. Because a heart that's open doesn't hide from life. It embraces it. Not carelessly – but completely. It leans into what feels true. It seeks not just to exist, but to grow, to become. To move with purpose, not abandon. And maybe that's what called me to try again. Not foolishness, but faith. That life has more to offer, if only we remember that a meaningful life requires us to act, not just dream.

"Now tell me…

"Do you think I sat down quietly like a sensible man and listened to my wife? Did I vow to never do something so ridiculous again?

"Of course not!

"I was going to do it again. How could I not? I mean, once you've tasted that kind of thrill, once you've felt like a falcon in the sky – well, you don't just give that up because of a little… ah… Disagreement. Oh no, I wasn't ready to back down. Not yet. A little more planning, a few adjustments, and next time…

"I'd soar all the way over the city!"

IX

"I set out to fly once more, driven by a single purpose: to glide above our bakery and let my wife witness it herself. At last, she would believe me. She'd have no choice then, would she? This time, I prepared more carefully. And yes – I even planned the landing. I chose the grand Crescent Tower. That towering relic, keeping watch over Al-Waadi, its eyes on every laughter-filled street and grief-shadowed

corner below. From there, I'd have a view of the river, glinting just beyond the city walls – the perfect course over the bakery and if needed, a forgiving place to fall. The tower casts its shadow wide across the city, and I knew it would give me the height I needed. I planned to fly just before sunset, when the winds soften and the light turns gentle. And I thought to myself: *If things go amiss, then at least the river may welcome me more kindly than the forest did!*

"I strapped on my newly crafted wings, pulling each buckle tight, even though I'd already done it four or five times. Still, I checked again. The wind was already tugging at the fabric, eager to carry me somewhere, anywhere. The city stretched out beneath me, distant and dreamlike. I could even make out our bakery, a tiny speck among the rooftops. My heart thundered with excitement, and my mind whispered, just leap. She'll see you, gliding above her head like a bird, and then she'll know.

"I took a deep breath and clutched the straps of my wings. This was it. This time, I had to convince myself. After all, I had barely survived the last attempt. The earth rising fast in a blur, the bone-shattering thud that nearly was, and the miracle of branches that caught me just in time. The memory still clung to every scar and every bruise. So why leap again?

"Because maybe this time would be different. Maybe I'd prepared enough. Maybe belief was enough. A thought circled around me like a tempting scent: *What if I could really fly?*

"As far as I knew, I'd be the first man to do it. No one in all the great cities of Al-Waadi had dared such a thing. Imagine the stories that would follow –

"The baker who soared above the rooftops, who'd pushed the limits of what anyone thought was possible. A feat worthy of legend. A strange sensation washed over me. Not fear, but something fiercer. A purpose so strong, it felt as though it might lift me already. As if the wind had leaned in, and whispered its encouragement. And wasn't it worth the risk? One chance to reach beyond the ordinary, to touch something greater than the days I'd come to accept. If I could do this, truly soar – it would mean something.

"To my wife. To my neighbours. To myself. Proof that I wasn't just a man who dreamed. I was the man who dared. I took a final breath, steadying my nerves. Above, the sky stretched wide and waiting. Below, the city shimmered – distant, delicate, like a dream within reach.

"In that moment, I knew. There was no turning back. I remember how in that single, suspended moment before I leapt, an astonishing thought came to me. A thought that seemed to slow time itself.

"Isn't it remarkable what a person can achieve when they truly set their mind to something?

"History, they say, is filled with those who dared to believe in what others thought impossible. Mighty empires rising from dust, great ships sailing uncharted seas, vast deserts crossed by nothing but will and conviction. None of those feats began with certainty or strength. They began with belief. Foolish, stubborn, extraordinary belief. It made me wonder, perhaps the true limits of a soul aren't defined by strength or skill, but by the courage to believe. How often does a person's own doubt keep them from all they could have achieved, when all it takes is the courage to move forward? If I could truly believe, with every fibre of my being, that I could conquer the skies...

"Then perhaps, just perhaps, the skies would yield. I had taken the time, after all, to prepare myself. Crafted my wings. Studied the winds. Chosen my path. The only thing that stood between me and success now, was my belief. And so, I did it.

"I leapt.

"With every ounce of conviction in my chest. Every mad, wild bit of determination I possessed. And then – the most remarkable thing happened. I began to fly. The wind caught beneath my wings; steady and sure, lifting me from the earth. I was soaring – truly soaring – above the city of Al-Waadi. For a heartbeat, the world was mine to command. The city beneath me, distant and small, almost unreal. The people below – their faces mere dots – they pointed, staring skywards, trying to make sense of the mad shape in the sky.

"Me. Flying. Like a fable coming to life. Exhilaration coursed through my veins. I had done it!

"I was flying. Truly flying.

"But then, as if fate itself had intervened, a sudden gust of wind struck me from the side. The force of it veered me off course, my wings shuddered and my body twisted in the air. I flapped, desperate to find balance, to wrest back control. But it was slipping fast. I had planned everything: to pass right over the bakery, let her see me with her own eyes, then glide down to the river like a leaf on a breeze. But the wind, fickle and free, had other plans. I had misjudged the distance. The river now seemed far behind me – shrinking, unreachable. Something clenched in my chest; not fear from the fall but the sudden clarity of my own foolishness. There would be no river at the end of this to soften this descent, nor would there be a forest to break my fall. I was racing straight into the city's heart, and the truth of my miscalculation surged through me faster than the drop itself. The rooftops rose to meet me, hard and painful. A rising blur of rooftops. I was no longer flying towards glory; I was falling into the city. I had soared too high. And now, it seemed the ground was ready to take me back. Unless, I found a miracle on the way down. And just as I braced myself for a rather unfortunate end, something extraordinary happened. Fate – perhaps amused by my madness – decided to intervene. I didn't meet stone. I didn't shatter on some unforgiving rooftop. Instead, with a tremendous splash…

"I landed in what I think might be the courtyard pool of the grand palace.

"Either by fate or fortune, who knows!

"I could hardly say which had saved me…

Part III

Rising Together

I

The Vizier stood motionless, as if sculpted from the very darkness that seemed to cling to him like a second skin. He stroked his well-kept beard, a familiar gesture when deep in thought. Hassan's tale echoed in the Vizier's mind, its bizarre details unravelling everything he thought he knew. It was a complete jolt from fate. A wild twist he hadn't seen coming. And in that moment, the Vizier was forced to confront a truth he rarely allowed himself to acknowledge:

Not everything could be planned.

No matter how carefully he crafted every detail of his approach. The unpredictable nature of it all rattled him, tearing open the very fabric of his control, exposing how fragile even his most carefully constructed plots truly could be. *Was this plan, so delicately crafted, worth salvaging?* The thought troubled him. Failure, he believed, was a foreign concept – one that could never touch him. In his mind, everything was within his control: his plans, his words, his fate. The idea of anything slipping through his fingers seemed absurd to him, as if he were untouchable by any force but his own will. So then, what choice was left? Except to salvage the plan. There was no question in his mind. He would not allow this moment to slip through his fingers. To admit that the plan could crumble now, undone by a single misstep – a pouch lost, as though the plan had never mattered in the first place – was unthinkable. It was not the plot that mattered, he reminded himself, but the vision it served: his ascendancy, his rightful rule.

A man such as he did not bow to the whims of fate. Fate bent to him. The Vizier's mind churned, calculating, recalibrating, as though the loss of one piece in a game of chess could still be twisted into victory. Could the pouch be retrieved, and with it, his ambitions secured?

If not, then these two before him – Hassan, lost in confusion, and Zayd, standing tense and fearful, knowing full well the cost of his failure – would have to pay the price. Already, the penalty they'd deserve was being measured. Not as a means of reclaiming his success. No, it was about restoring his fractured control.

He needed to remind them, and himself, that his authority was absolute, and no mistake would go unpunished.

His thoughts, though seasoned with arrogance, carried a trace of something deeper – an unspoken fear. That the world might not mould itself to his will as he always thought. He had lived his life as a sculptor, shaping what was before him, moulding power and people to his desires. So, what was power if not a reflection of control? And what was control if it could be stolen by a pair of fumbling fools with nothing but desperation to offer?

A wise man, he mused silently, *knows when to exercise patience as his anchor and when to sever the chain that holds him back.*

He glanced at the two men, his dark eyes calculating their worth like a merchant appraising damaged goods. To recover the pouch might be to recover his plan, but to abandon it… to let it fall… was a dangerous gamble. What would remain, then, but the emptiness of failure?

For a moment, the Vizier considered the audacity of Hassan's tale. Wild. Unbelievable. And yet, there was no lie in those old eyes. The story was strange – yes. But in its strangeness lay its potential. It didn't matter that Hassan had done something impossible; what mattered was how the Vizier could twist this unexpected revelation to his advantage. A story like that could be a powerful tool. A distraction perhaps. Or it could be discarded. It was his to decide. The narrative was in his hands now, ready to be shaped to serve his needs. Or, if it proved useless, cut away without a second thought. Finally, he spoke.

"You have one day to bring me that pouch." The words were not just a command; they were a judgment, a proclamation of dominance. Patience as a blade, he reminded himself. It wasn't enough to simply wait – no.

Patience required control, discipline, like a blade poised for the perfect strike. He had no need for hasty action; the moment would come when the conditions were ripe, and then, he would act with precision, cutting away the obstacles before him.

"And you, Zayd," he added, his voice carrying a promise of quiet devastation.

"You lost the pouch."

"If it is not returned by the end of tomorrow, both of you will find yourselves paying for that mistake… in ways you cannot yet imagine."

With a final dismissive glance, he pushed past the two men, his very movement a reminder of the severity of his warning. The guards, without waiting for a command, fell in line behind him like shadows. They prodded Zayd and Hassan with the practiced force of shepherds driving a flock. Hassan shuffled beside Zayd, still oblivious to the full extent of the chaos he had fallen into. Zayd's fate balanced unsteadily on the fragile foundation of Hassan's story. Had the old man truly found the pouch? Or was this another cruel twist of fortune that would drag them both further into the Vizier's wrath? Anxiety twisted in Zayd's chest. Their survival – their chance to undo the chaos of the situation – rested entirely on Hassan. A strange old man lost in the absurdity of his own wild ambitions.

II

Outside the palace gates, the night unfolded like a calming tide, its quiet stillness washing away the tension that had clung to them within those suffocating walls. Zayd moved with purpose. His only focus: retrieve the pouch and resolve this looming crisis. Beside him, however, strolled Hassan – a stark contrast to Zayd's determined energy. He walked as if carried by a breeze, his thoughts alight with wonder, untouched by the Vizier's warning or the significance of their predicament. Hassan had no idea just how dangerous the Vizier truly was. Beyond the palace walls, to those who had never encountered him personally, the Vizier carried an unblemished reputation. He was the Sultan's most trusted hand. A symbol of wisdom and loyalty, his name spoken with respect throughout the kingdom. Even Hassan's understanding of him came from the glowing words of others: tales of his sharp intellect, steadfast service, and calm demeanour.

But Zayd knew better.

Beneath the Vizier's polished exterior lay greed, corruption, and ambition so sharp it could sever anything in its path. The man's carefully cultivated image was a lie, and Zayd had seen enough to know the truth. The Vizier wasn't a friend of the Sultan, but a danger to the kingdom itself.

"Did you see him?" Hassan burst out; his eyes wide with excitement.

"The Vizier! What a presence! And his voice – did you hear it?"

"Wow! It was like stones dropping into a river, each word carried so much weight." He waved his arms as if trying to capture the energy of the moment.

To Hassan, their encounter seemed like a grand moment of fortune rather than the deadly warning it truly was. Zayd stopped abruptly and turned to face him. His voice seemed steady but it was wrapped in frustration.

"How can you stand here in awe of a man who has just threatened to kill us?" Hassan blinked, startled.

"What, that? Oh, no, no – that was nothing! The Vizier just has a way about him. He's very direct, that's all. I've heard plenty about him from people – "

"Well, let me tell you about him as someone who sees him every day," Zayd cut in.

"That 'way about him' is a mask. If you don't get that pouch to him, Hassan, he will kill us both."

Hassan's smile faded, the brightness in his eyes dimming for the first time as doubt crept into his expression. Zayd pressed on.

"You speak of majesty, and yet you ignore the danger, Hassan. It won't be stones sinking. It will be us."

Hassan scratched his head, glancing away as though trying to dismiss the thought. Perhaps Zayd was right. After all, the Vizier's obsession with what seemed like a worthless pouch made little sense. What could be inside it that would lead a man so powerful to resort to such threats? Zayd didn't wait for him to respond.

"The pouch is more important than you know. The Vizier had me retrieve it from a magician.

"And magicians… we both know, aren't meddled with unless there's dark intent behind it." He let the silence stretch between them, allowing the truth to sink in.

"I believe the Vizier plans to poison the Sultan. That pouch – it holds the poison." Zayd's eyes bore into Hassan relentlessly, as though he could force the truth into his mind with nothing but his stare.

"I've seen it – ominous men, slipping in and out of the palace. I can't be sure they're dangerous, but their very presence makes me uneasy."

"I have heard things too, things that perhaps I shouldn't have. He thinks I am invisible. Just a servant. But I've heard enough. I know what he's planning."

Hassan swallowed. His wild, comical nature had momentarily been set aside, eclipsed by the importance of Zayd's words. Hassan understood. What seemed like a strange adventure now loomed with deadly seriousness. Zayd continued, focused as ever.

"What comes next is simple. We go to your home. We find the pouch – if it's even the right one – and then we figure out how to survive this."

Upon hearing this, Hassan let out a soft snuffle, half amusement, half surprise at what he had just heard.

"Surviving, Zayd? Why settle for that? What if this – this – is our chance to act? Fate has opened the door, and it's not for us to stand by while evil circles the Sultan. Maybe we're not passengers, my friend. Maybe we're here to change the course of this story."

Despite the enigmatic nature of Hassan, his words resonated with surprising clarity. Zayd realised he may have underestimated this man. For Hassan, perhaps this call to action sprang from an adventurous spirit, a yearning for excitement. But for Zayd, those words struck deeper, igniting a spark of possibility within him – *maybe this wasn't just about surviving after all*. For so long, he had been adrift, carried by the current of life's cruel hand. His ambitions drowned beneath his own sorrows. Each day had felt like a slow sinking – caught between what could never be changed and what he feared he would never achieve. But Hassan's fire... It lit something deep within him. What if this was it? Zayd wondered. What if fate, however unkind, had brought him to this very moment, not to endure passively, but to act? He remembered the famous story in Al-Waadi, a tale passed from lips to ears over countless moonlit gatherings.

It was a story of a man taken by bandits and thrown into a dungeon deep in the desert, his fate sealed – or so he believed. Days blurred into weeks. Despair became his only companion. Yet what he did not know was that the Sultan's army had long since defeated his captors, scattering them into the sands. One day, a passing traveller heard faint cries from the dungeon. Cu-

rious, he opened the door, finding the man slumped in the corner,
frail but alive.

"Why have you not left?" the traveller asked. The man, be-
wildered, replied,

"I thought I was still imprisoned."

The traveller's response echoed in Zayd's memory, as
crisp as if it had been spoken to him:

"Your fear was the only chain you bore. The moment you
would have chosen to pursue freedom, you would have been free."

Perhaps Zayd's own prison had no bars after all. This
was not the end of his story, but the beginning of something entirely new. He had always thought of this tale as
a simple fable, shared to entertain or offer a momentary
lesson. Yet now, it felt deeply personal. How long could
a man remain bound before he dared to break free? The
chains that held him weren't made of iron – they were
imagined, woven from doubts, fears, and the deceptive
comfort of inaction disguised as helplessness. Was he, too,
sitting behind an open door? Zayd realised this fable was
about the imagined barriers that hold us back – prisons
built from fear and doubt, strengthened by the belief that
escape is impossible. But the truth was simpler: a better
life, something beyond the false comfort of the dungeon,
might already be waiting. It wouldn't come by chance or

rescue. It would come only through action – by rising, reaching, daring to push open the door. Freedom and the chance for something greater, could never be guaranteed. But it would never be within reach if he didn't take the first step.

For the first time in a long while, Zayd wondered: *What if the power to change his fate had always been within his grasp – if only he would take it?*

III

Hassan's house was as modest as the man himself, tucked just off the busy street where his bakery thrived. Its simplicity was reflected in the quiet hum of the neighbourhood, where the aroma of fresh bread lingered in the air, mingling with the dust and the last traces of the day's bustle. The street had quietened now, the night settling in, but whispers of an extraordinary sight – a man soaring through the skies over Al-Waadi – had begun to ripple through the neighbourhood.

Hassan's wife had heard the murmurs, the neighbours' bewildered exclamations drifting through the open window. She didn't need their gossip to confirm what her heart already knew. It had to be Hassan. Who else could dream

up such reckless, audacious madness? But if it was him –
where was he now? Her hands, usually steady, trembled
as she adjusted a clay jug on the counter. Her mind racing.
Her foolish, wonderful husband – what had he done this
time? For all her irritation with his wild aspirations, she
knew one thing: she couldn't bear to lose him. Had his
yearning for something greater – a life beyond the flour-
streaked walls of his bakery – led him to ruin? Images of
him falling, broken, somewhere in the city flooded her
thoughts, and she swallowed hard against the rising tide
of fear. The man she loved, with all his absurd ideas and
boundless optimism, could not have met such an end. But
what if he had? Her pacing stopped as she turned sharply
towards the door. Its silence felt unbearable, as though it
mocked her with its stillness, withholding the answers she
desperately needed but feared to hear. She pressed a hand
to her temple, closing her eyes against the sting of tears
that threatened to spill.

"Oh God, bring him back to me."

Then – the silence shattered. The door burst open with
a loud thud, slamming against the wall and rattling the entire room. She froze, her heart leaping as a familiar voice
rang out.

"My love!" Hassan proclaimed with delight, stepping into the room as though he had merely returned from a stroll.

His arms flung wide, his grin so impossibly wide it could have split his face.

"Did you *see* it? Did you see me?!" He twirled dramatically.

"Flying! Like an eagle – no, a falcon! *The Hawk of Al-Waadi!* That's what they'll call me!"

Her mouth fell open, her emotions colliding in a whirlwind of relief, fury, and disbelief. She took one deliberate step towards him, planting her hands firmly on her hips, unleashing a glare that could melt stone.

"Hassan!" she screamed, trembling with barely restrained anger.

"I swear by the heavens above, I should kill you myself! At least then I'd know where you are!"

Hassan blinked, startled, before his grin returned. He placed a hand on his chest.

"Kill me? My love, I've already stared death in the face and made it back to you. Can't we just be glad I'm here?"

"This is no joke!" She snapped. "My heart was in turmoil, wondering what had become of you. I heard murmurs of a man flying!"

"Flying!"

"And who else could it have been but you? And of course, no sign of you all day!

"Do you even care if you live or die?"

He softened slightly, stepping closer.

"I –"

"You don't!" she interrupted. "If you did, you wouldn't do these ridiculous things!"

"You have gone too far this time, Hassan. Too far."

"What if you'd fallen? What if I was left alone, mourning you while the city whispered about how foolish you were?"

"Foolish?" Hassan echoed, as though deeply offended.

"I flew. *Flew!* Does that sound foolish to you? Or does it sound... miraculous?"

"It sounds reckless!" she shot back, her cheeks flushed with emotion. Do you even think about me, about us, before you go chasing after these absurd dreams of yours?"

Hassan paused, then smiled again. His voice dropped into a smooth, almost playful tone, trying to win her over.

"Of course I think of you. You are the fire that drives me, the reason I reach for the impossible. Aren't you proud? I might just be the first person to have ever flown, the first to achieve the impossible."

"Proud?" she repeated, unconvinced. "Proud that my husband might have turned himself into a smear on the ground?" She shook her head, exasperated.

"Hassan, *you* are impossible."

"And yet," he said, stepping closer, "you love me all the same."

Her glare wavered. Just for a moment, she sighed heavily.

"You can't keep doing this, Hassan. I mean it.

"This... this was too much. You have made your point, whatever it was. Let it end here."

"Ah, but that's where you're wrong, my flower. It wasn't about making a point – it was to prove something. You said I couldn't fly. You said it was impossible. You chuckled at my dreams. And yet here I am, standing before you, a man who has done the impossible."

She threw her hands up in frustration.

"So, you've proven me wrong. Fine. Are you happy now?"

He nodded. "Very. But more importantly, I think I have lived enough for a lifetime in that single moment. And I promise, no more flying. No more chasing the impossible."

"You mean it?"

"I do," he said, placing a hand over his heart.

"For now, my love…" He gestured towards the doorway. "…a new adventure has found me. One I didn't seek but must see through."

She turned, her eyes landing on this stranger for the first time. Perhaps her anger had blinded her to his presence. He stood awkwardly in the doorway, his expression tense and uncertain, as if he were intruding on something intensely personal.

"Allow me to introduce Zayd."

"Zayd," Hassan said with exaggerated flourish, "this is my beloved wife, Yasmin, the most remarkable woman in all of Al-Waadi."

She hesitated for a moment, her anger dissipating like mist in the morning sun, transforming into a warm smile as she stepped towards Zayd.

"You'll forgive my outburst," she said, a hint of embarrassment colouring her cheeks.

Her tone softened, now gentle and welcoming.

"Welcome." Her natural hospitality swiftly took over, guiding Zayd inside with a graceful gesture.

"Come in, sit. I'll prepare something," she offered, her voice brightening as she tried to shift the mood, eager to extend kindness despite her earlier frustration.

IV

Zayd's leg bounced restlessly where he sat. His fingers drummed against the edge of his knee, tapping out a frantic rhythm as if trying to beat back the surge of anxiety.

"Hassan," he snapped. "Have you found it yet?"

Hassan, bent over a small chest in the corner, muttered something indistinct as he rummaged through its contents. Zayd leaned forward, his elbows digging into his knees, hands clasped tightly as if holding himself together. His eyes darted towards the doorway, then back to Hassan, as though expecting danger to appear at any moment.

"Hurry!" Zayd said, panicked. "It's not just a pouch, Hassan. You know that. Every second we waste – "

Hassan raised a hand without turning.

"I'm looking, Zayd. It's here somewhere." Then a triumphant cry:

"Haah!"

After what felt like an eternity, Hassan presented the pouch to Zayd. Zayd snatched it almost before Hassan could extend it. His fingers almost trembling with anticipation. He didn't open it – he couldn't yet – but his eyes inspected every fold, every stitch, every detail. His heart raced as he recognised the familiar shape, the way it felt in his hands. A wave of relief washed over him. This was it – the pouch he had lost. Closing his eyes, Zayd allowed himself a rare breath of peace. The nightmare of the past few days had finally come to an end. Or so he thought. His focus sharpened once more, and he glanced at Hassan, urgency flashing in his eyes.

"Let's go Hassan. We have to get back to the palace, now."

As Zayd turned towards the door, Hassan's wife entered carrying a steaming pot of tea, her presence warm and friendly.

"Where are you rushing off to?" she asked softly.

"Sit for a moment," she urged. "I have just prepared tea. A moment's rest won't harm you."

Zayd hesitated for a moment, caught between the urgency of the task ahead and the kindness in her invitation. The severity of the situation pulled at him, but her gentle hospitality, the warmth of the room, the sweet scent of the tea – it all felt so welcoming. With a reluctant sigh, he let the urgency of the moment slip away for just a heartbeat. He sat, his shoulders easing slightly as he allowed himself this brief break. Hassan's wife poured the tea. Her hands were steady, her presence calming in a way Zayd hadn't realised he needed.

"Thank you," he murmured. It was a small comfort, but in that moment, it was enough.

"It's late now, and the streets will be dark. Why not stay the night?"

Zayd hesitated, his thoughts a tangled mess, but her presence was soothing, like a balm on his weary soul. Something about her reminded him of his mother – her voice, tender yet firm, carrying the depth of care. He felt an instant warmth, a sense of being welcomed, as though he belonged here, even in his uncertainty. Zayd glanced towards Hassan, who offered a quick, knowing smile, clearly not eager to leave either. His reluctance was softened by her kindness and he found himself nodding.

"Fine…I'll go tomorrow with Hassan." He gave in, his heart lightened by her generosity.

She smiled.

"Tomorrow, then," she said, pouring the tea.

After a while, as they sipped their tea and exchanged quiet conversation, the atmosphere softened, the tension of the night easing with each word. Yasmin, noticing the young man's deepening weariness, kept the conversation light, coaxing him into revealing small fragments of his guarded life. Then, as if a memory stirred in her, she paused, her expression thoughtful before she spoke again.

"I knew your mother, Zayd," she said suddenly.

"She used to come by the bakery occasionally, her face always so bright. She always spoke of you – so proud. She said you worked harder than any boy she knew."

Zayd looked up, surprised, but a soft sadness filled his chest.

"Yes... she always wanted the best for me."

Yasmin studied him for a moment.

"Your mother always spoke of your ambitions, how you burned with determination to fulfil your dreams. I believe... she would still be proud."

"Why the palace, Zayd?" she asked, her words carrying no judgment, only quiet curiosity. She let the question hang, giving him space to answer.

Zayd looked away for a moment, discomfort swirling in him. He was reluctant to talk about it, unsure of how to answer.

"I wanted to be a judge," he said. "That was our dream. To study, to earn my place, to change things for the better." He paused, swallowing down the ache in his throat.

"But... I couldn't finish my studies. Not enough coin. No one to help. The palace... it was the next best thing. A place close to the courtrooms. Close to where I imagined myself standing one day."

He laughed bitterly under his breath.

"If I couldn't be what I wanted... at least I could be near it. It felt better than letting go completely."

"Change things for the better?" she echoed.

She looked right through him, as though she could see through the veil of his well-constructed exterior.

"I suppose not," Zayd said quietly. "I'm not sure where I'm going anymore."

Hassan trying to lift the mood, chimed in.

"Oh, don't listen to him, he's just trying to make sense of all this. The Vizier, plotting to poison the Sultan? It sounds like a story told by wandering bards. The palace – a bastion of justice and power – is the last place one would expect such treachery. Yet, here we are, questioning the very heart of the kingdom."

Zayd's eyes widened. "Hassan!"

He glanced nervously at Yasmin and then over his shoulder. Hassan's wife remained calm, though a glimmer of concern passed across her face.

"Poison the Sultan?" she repeated softly. "Why would anyone...?"

Zayd leaned forward, lowering his voice.

"The Vizier... he's dangerous. I've seen him meet with suspicious people. I don't know everything, but I believe the pouch...this pouch holds the poison."

Yasmin paused, her hands resting lightly in her lap, fingers interlacing absentmindedly. She tilted her head slightly, her gaze drifting to the floor as a moment of stillness enveloped her. The hush deepened, yet the room felt alive with unspoken thoughts. When she finally spoke, she carefully assessed each word before allowing them to escape.

"You know," her voice was calm, yet it carried the essence of reflection.

"I've been reflecting on destiny."

"With all of Hassan's wild talk about it, I can't help but wonder if fate isn't just about the events that unfold around us. It's also about how we respond to them."

"Perhaps this is your moment, Zayd. Not merely to exist, but to become a force for good."

"Fate doesn't present us with opportunities like this without a purpose. It challenges us to rise, to act, and to shape our lives."

Zayd listened, his breath catching in his chest, the words striking deeper than he expected. Yasmin continued.

"Sometimes, it's not about the path we imagined walking. It's about the one that unfolds before us. When that moment arrives, we have a choice: to step forward and embrace it, or to let it pass by, leaving our story unfinished."

He remembered the ambition he had once held – to be a judge, to spread justice, to do what was right. This was not the way he had imagined making a difference, but... could it still be the path to fulfilling his purpose? Not in the courts. Not in the title. But by action. By bringing light into the darkness the Vizier sought to cast.

"We need a plan!" Zayd said, his voice no longer clouded by hesitation.

"What's there to plan?" Hassan shrugged.

"If you think it's poison, let's dispose of it – toss it in the river. Simple."

Zayd shook his head.

"It's not that simple, Hassan. If we destroy it outright, the Vizier won't let us walk away...We need a replacement – something identical, but harmless."

Yasmin cut in, calm and practical.

"Hold on."

"There's no sense crafting a grand plan over a mystery. Open the pouch. See what you are dealing with first."

Hassan rolled his eyes but reached for the pouch resting on the table. He tossed it into Zayd's hands.

"Fine. Let's see what we're dealing with."

Zayd hesitated, the pouch feeling alive in his hands, as if it pulsed with hidden purpose. His fingers worked at the knotted cord, slow and deliberate, as if untying it might unleash something far greater than poison. Even

Hassan, usually brimming with mischief, watched quietly, caught in the stillness of the moment. The pouch opened with a faint rustle, so what was inside? A cloud of cursed dust strong enough to turn them all to ash. Perhaps an insect, bewitched and deadly, ready to sink its fangs into whoever dared disturb it.

No.

It contained...seeds. Small, unassuming seeds, as plain as any you'd find in a farmer's satchel. Was that what the Vizier was so eager to get his hands on? For a long moment, no one spoke. Then Hassan threw back his head and laughed.

"Seeds!"

"The Vizier's grand, deadly secret is...seeds?

"Zayd, you had me bracing for something more sinister."

Zayd's cheeks flushed, humiliated.

"I was sure it was poison," he muttered, pouring the seeds onto the table.

Yasmin, ever steady, said softly, "we can't be too quick to judge, things aren't always as they seem. We don't yet know what they might do."

She spoke partly to ease Zayd's embarrassment – after all, he had convinced them all the pouch held something far more menacing – and partly out of her own quiet caution. Anything the Vizier sought so carefully was not to be taken so lightly. Whatever the seeds were, they had been worth a great deal of effort to conceal, and that alone made them worth considering carefully. Hassan, growing restless, flicked a seed across the floor. It landed near a mouse that had been skittering at the edges of the room. The rodent paused, sniffing the tiny object before nibbling at it, its small paws moving with quick, eager motions. The mouse's movements slowed. But then, for a moment, everything was still. Its eyes glazed over. Its body trembled and collapsed in a limp heap, the faintest squeak escaping its mouth before all was silent. Zayd stared at the pouch in horror, his earlier embarrassment now replaced with grim certainty. Slowly, they all looked at each other – the same realisation dawning in each of their eyes.

"It is poison," Zayd said at last.

Yasmin turned to Zayd, her gaze unwavering and fierce.

"Then the path is clear. Destroy them. Replace them. Do whatever must be done, but you must not let this evil take root."

V

Each new morning is a testament to the quiet resilience of the world, a gentle assurance that even after the deepest darkness, light will return. It whispers that yesterday's troubles belong to yesterday, and the brisk air serves as more than a wake-up call. It is a reminder to rise not just from slumber, but from the belief that we cannot shape new possibilities today. With each new dawn comes the quiet power to begin again, to change not only our lives, but perhaps the world itself. And yet, as the light unfolds around us, how often do we truly pause to see it?

Hassan and Zayd walked side by side, their footsteps muffled by the stillness of the hour. The world felt suspended between the shadows of the night and the promise of the day. Neither spoke. Yet their silence pulsed – not with emptiness, but with unvoiced fears and plans still waiting to take shape. Each step forward carried a sense of urgency laced with futility, as if the enormity of what lay ahead threatened to consume them before they could act. Yasmin had seen them off with the words that stayed with Zayd like seeds planted deep in his heart.

"You may not have chosen this path," she said softly, standing in the doorway, her eyes steady and calm as the dawn.

"But perhaps it chose you. Trust that there's a reason you're here, Zayd.

"Sometimes, the road to what's right doesn't announce itself – it unfolds as you walk it. Believe in that and believe in yourself."

She stepped back, the faintest smile touching her lips – a smile that said she already knew he would. As they approached the towering palace gates, Hassan's usual buoyant stride had vanished. Each step measured, as though he were treading on uncertain ground. The murmur of palace life filtered through the morning air, distant and subdued, like a world they were no longer a part of. Zayd's gaze lingered on the gates, their imposing structure a threshold to the unknown. Every footfall felt like a question, each step an unspoken wager – was this the moment the doors to triumph would open, or would they find themselves lost in a maze of peril? The palace loomed ahead, and with it, a quiet reluctance crept into their steps, each one slower than the last. A guard stepped forward, his face offered no clue to his thoughts. He gave Zayd a brief glance, then turned to Hassan.

"Only you, baker," the guard said, crossing his arms with an authority that brooked no argument.

"The Vizier requests you alone. The young man," he nodded at Zayd, "is to return to his duties. The Vizier wishes to speak with you, and you only."

Hassan hesitated, his eyes darting towards Zayd before shifting to the guard.

"Only me?" he repeated, uncertain.

The guard remained impassive.

"The Vizier's orders are clear. Only you."

Zayd stepped forward smoothly, masking his unease.

"No need for you to trouble yourself. I will take him," he offered lightly.

"I know the way well enough. Besides, you have your post here." The words were casual – but beneath them ran a hidden urgency. Zayd knew this moment mattered. The fact that the Vizier wanted to see him alone; he needed just a few more steps with Hassan – one last exchange – to ensure the Vizier's influence would not take root. The guard shook his head firm, as though the matter was already settled.

"You will not. The Vizier's instructions are clear. The baker goes alone. You…are to return to your duties."

Zayd hesitated, a flare of frustration rising in his chest, but he knew there was no room for defiance. The guard's mind was made up. In the palace, Zayd was still just a servant. Hassan adjusted his tunic with a deliberate tug, straightening his posture as if armouring himself.

"Not to worry," he said, whilst keeping his tone light, though his words came just a little too quickly.

"This is nothing. I'll see to it and find you after." He gave a faint shrug, as if brushing off any concern, but the feeling in his stomach betrayed him.

Zayd watched as Hassan followed the guard, until they turned a corner and were out of sight. His steps seemed steady but his heavy breathing suggested tension. Zayd's thoughts wandered to a parable his mother told him long ago.

A tale of a traveller crossing a barren desert with a flask for water and a satchel of gold. Day after day, the traveller trudged under the unrelenting sun, the gold growing heavier with each step. His thirst troubled him, but he clung to the treasure, unwilling to surrender it. When he finally reached an oasis, his hands trembled from exhaustion, too weak to lift the flask to his lips. The gold, once precious, became the weight that buried him in the shifting sands.

As the parable faded from his mind, Zayd's thoughts circled back to Hassan and the choice before him. What was the price of a man? Was it his loyalty? His integrity? Or the dreams of something greater than the world had ever offered him? Surely, the Vizier would tempt Hassan with promises. Wealth. Prestige. Comfort. It would seem so easy to accept. Easy to trade their purpose for riches. Easy to cling to the shiny offer and forget the thirst that had driven them here. The thirst to save the kingdom.

Would Hassan see it?

Would he recognise that the gold the Vizier offered could bury him just as surely as it had the traveller? Every compromise, every small surrender, would drag him further from his purpose – just as the traveller, clutching his gold, had forgotten his own survival until it was too late. The road paved with riches was a mirage, shimmering over empty sands. The real road – the one that could change everything – could only be walked through sacrifice: the courage to let go of what we want, in order to reach what we need.

Part IV

As It Was Meant...

I

H*assan stepped into the Vizier's chamber, the heavy doors* closing behind him with a quiet finality. A delicate wisp of incense drifted through the air, a fragile veil that failed to mask the room's underlying menace. His eyes swept the room – vast and opulent, yet suffocating in its grandeur. Richly woven drapes covered the walls, their intricate patterns dancing subtly in the flickering light. A long table stretched across the centre of the room, surrounded by elaborately carved chairs, but all attention was drawn to the man seated at the far end. The Vizier sat with an air of command, as if the room itself revolved around him. Draped in rich silken robes, he rested one hand on the arm of his chair tapping his fingers in a steady rhythm. His sharp, watchful eyes were locked on Hassan, a subtle smile on his lips – too elusive to reveal if it was welcoming or cruel. Hassan stepped forward; the pouch cradled in both hands like a fragile relic. His voice trembled as he spoke, each word cautious and tight with nerves.

"As you asked, respected Vizier. I – I didn't want to disappoint."

For a heartbeat, the Vizier remained still. Then, like a mask lifting, his features softened. A warm chuckle escaped him.

"Disappoint?" he repeated, with amusement. "My dear Hassan, you've exceeded my expectations." The sudden shift in his tone was so effortless, so inviting, the tension of the moment slipped away. Hassan caught off guard, let a smile break.

"I have always said, a baker's hands are skilled not only for bread but for all manner of tasks." He laughed lightly. "Though, truth be told, my hands are better suited to running errands for men like you – more so than for shaping loaves of bread."

The Vizier leaned back, a low hum of approval rising from his throat.

"Indeed, my friend," he said. "As we know, your talents are far more than mere baking. Few could have handled such responsibility so capably."

Hassan raised his chin, a sense of pride washing over him.

"If only my wife could hear your praise," joked Hassan, the sound of his glee echoing through the chamber. His nerves were forgotten under the Vizier's disarming charm. The Vizier smiled, but behind his courteous mask, patience waited. The patience of a hunter watching a trapped animal tire itself out. Taking command of the conversation, the Vizier spoke.

"Extraordinary actions," his tone shifting, drawing Hassan in deeper, "are like sparks that leap from a fire, carried by the wind. To the untrained eye, they are but fleeting flickers, barely noticed before they vanish. Yet to those who know how to watch – those who understand their true worth – such sparks hold the potential to ignite new flames. They can be nurtured into a blaze of opportunity."

He paused, allowing the words to settle, then shifted closer, his intent clear.

"Your flight, Hassan, was one such spark. A moment that one cannot ignore. And now, the Sultan himself has taken notice. He has heard of your remarkable feat…"

Hassan's face lit up.

"Tonight…" The Vizier added. "I am inviting you to the royal banquet. I want the Sultan to hear the tale from your own lips – among his nobles, no less. A rare chance, wouldn't you say?"

Ideas sparked and collided in Hassan's mind. Too fast. Too bright to catch. He imagined himself standing before the Sultan, recounting his flight, seeing the wonder in the eyes of those who had gathered to listen.

This is it, he thought. *This is what happens when you dare to take the first step – when you decide to leap into the unknown.* For a brief moment, he was lost in the fantasy of it all – the room full of nobles, the Sultan's face captivated with attention, the thrill of seeing it all unfold. *I'll be a hero*, he thought, *a legend*. The more he thought about it, the more the edges of his purpose blurred. The change he had sought – to protect the Sultan, to foil the Vizier's plan – seemed distant now, almost irrelevant compared to the allure of this new path unfolding before him. There were no whispers of poison, no dangerous seeds to be swapped, only the chance to tell a tale. A story that could elevate him to heights he had never imagined.

I've done it, he thought. *I took the risk, and now the world is waiting for me.* The Vizier's words wrapped around him like a warm cloak, soothing his doubts. The reward of his courage, his extraordinary action, was being handed to him on a silver platter. *What was it they said?* Hassan thought absently. *A closed door only opens for the hand that dares to knock.*

The world was rewarding his bravery, as if the very fabric of fate had shifted in his favour. And why not? Surely this was the way things were meant to unfold. After all, hadn't he earned it? Somewhere deep inside, a flicker of doubt stirred – a faint echo of Zayd's warnings – but Hassan barely heard it over the roaring tide of hope and excitement. And so, with a grin that seemed a little too wide, he nodded to the Vizier.

"Tonight then," he said, almost breathless from the excitement.

"I'll be there, ready to share my story with the Sultan himself."

The Vizier's gaze shifted to the pouch in his hand, his fingers caressing its surface as if weighing the significance of the contents within. Then, slowly, his eyes lifted to meet Hassan's.

"You have done well, Hassan."

Beneath his words of praise, there was an unmistakable calculation at work. Hassan's excitement, his eagerness to please, had made the perfect opening. And now, with the spark of anticipation still glowing in Hassan's eyes, the Vizier could work his magic. The bait had been set, and the hook was already embedded.

"Please, sit," he said, his invitation conveying a sense of intimacy, as though they were about to share a confidence.

"We have much to discuss. Such extraordinary actions deserve a more thorough conversation."

Hassan, still riding the high of the attention and the promise of greater things to come, stepped forward without hesitation, taking the seat the Vizier gestured to. There was no thought of suspicion, only the thrill of being in the company of such power. But the Vizier, ever the master of control, saw this as the perfect moment to tighten his grip on the situation. The Vizier knew he needed to ensure no loose ends were left. The real task, now that Hassan was entranced, was to carefully extract the information he needed – the final pieces of the puzzle that would secure his own plans.

"Tell me," continued the Vizier smoothly.

"What truly drove you, Hassan?"

"Men do not risk everything without reason – and ambition alone is never the whole story."

The Vizier's words flowed easily, designed to flatter, to draw Hassan, without revealing the hook beneath the bait. He wasn't just a man of power; he was a master of manipulation, pulling the strings of Hassan's desires. Hassan, warmed by the Vizier's easy tone, rushed to answer – eager, unguarded, spilling words before caution could catch them. He mistook the Vizier's interest for genuine admiration, and with that small, fatal comfort, he began to ramble – unaware that the Vizier was already steering the conversation towards a single purpose: to test him, to see if his carelessness would reveal any truth worth knowing.

He did not know if there was something to uncover – but Hassan's wildness, his impulsive spirit, made him a tempting thread to tug on. He needed to be sure. Hassan spoke of courage, of dreams, of risks taken – but the Vizier, masked in patient silence listened only with half an ear. Hassan's voice was little more than a murmur at the edges of his thoughts. His mind churned, busy with calculation, evaluating possibilities, considering what truths might yet be teased free. Then, smoothly, the Vizier cut across Hassan's words – not rudely, but with the subtlety of a man steering a conversation without resistance.

"You know," he began, his voice slicing cleanly through the haze of Hassan's enthusiasm...

"There's an old saying about the truths we carry, and what it costs to keep them."

Hassan nodded absently, his words trailing off as the Vizier spoke over him. He watched Hassan intently, crafting each word with care.

"Imagine a man tasked with carrying a secret across a long and perilous road. He did not choose it; it was entrusted to him – a duty he cannot forsake without betraying himself or others. At first, the secret feels light enough."

"But the further he walks, the heavier it becomes – not because the secret itself has changed, but because the fear grows heavier."

"The longer he carries it, the more he dreads what might happen if he falters: one careless word, one crack in his resolve, and everything he has sworn to protect could unravel."

"The burden is not the secret alone, but the silence, the isolation, and the fear of failure that tighten around him with every step." The Vizier's eyes glinted, thoughtful, as if he spoke not just to Hassan, but to something deeper inside him.

"And then, along the road, he meets a guide – someone who sees the weariness in him. Someone who offers to lift the burden from his soul. 'Trust me,' the guide says. 'Lay it down, and be free.'" The Vizier smiled, slow and subtle.

"Many would say yes. Of course they would. Who would not choose freedom over fear?" He let the moment stretch, then added softly, "and yet... when the moment comes, so few do. They cling to their burden, even as it grinds them into the dust."

The Vizier's gaze held Hassan's, steady and knowing.

"I wonder, Hassan... why is that?"

Hassan shifted in his seat. He still heard the sizzle of excitement in his mind, the memory of the Vizier's invitation, the promise of something greater. The words swirled around him, gentle, tempting.

"The question is simple," the Vizier continued.

"But that choice…Perhaps it requires more than courage. It requires faith – faith that laying down the burden will not destroy him, but set him free."

"I… I am afraid I am not following, respected Vizier."

Hassan's thoughts scrambled, unease prickling under his skin, but the Vizier's calm, steady presence pulled him back, anchoring his mind before it could drift too far. The Vizier smiled faintly, a patient predator.

"I mean, my young baker, that the price of truth is often greater than we're willing to admit."

"We tell ourselves a secret can be kept – that silence will protect it. But the longer it lives, the more fragile it becomes. A moment of fear, a careless word, a glance at the wrong time...

And the truth slips free, beyond our grasp, carried by the whims of fate."

"But it does not have to come to that. Not all hands are careless. Sometimes, if trust is given wisely, a secret can be protected – held safe – while choice still belongs to you."

"The secret need not undo you. Not if you entrust it before it escapes."

Hassan swallowed; his throat dry. Behind the veil of words, he could see it now – the Vizier was not offering him wisdom. He was testing him. Feeling for cracks. Assessing whether the secret Hassan carried was still hidden – or if it had already slipped free. Hassan glimpsed at the pouch – still cradled loosely in the Vizier's hand – but his mind raced back to Zayd, to their plan, to the quiet, desperate hope they had pinned to secrecy. The Vizier's eyes never left him. Unblinking. Calculating. It was like a serpent coiling around him, the pressure of its constraint building the longer he remained silent.

"And now, Hassan, we arrive at the moment the man must choose." His words were soft, almost kind, but Hassan could hear the menace behind them.

"What will he do with his burden?"

"Will he risk everything to guard it?"

"Or will he place his trust where it might yet save him – and gain more than he ever imagined?"

Hassan bit his lip unconsciously, his heart pounding faster than it had when he tried to fly. The Vizier's patience, it seemed, was infinite – but his meaning was unmistakeable. A choice was being laid out before Hassan, but whichever path he chose, danger engulfed him. The Vizier tilted his head, studying him with polite curiosity – as if this was merely an academic question, of no great consequence. Then with a quiet finality, the serpent struck:

"Tell me Hassan. Did you open the pouch?"

For the first time, Hassan wondered if he had truly understood the man before him – or if he had been dancing, blindfolded, on the edge of a serpent's strike all along. He had been so caught up in the excitement of it all. The flight, the chance to meet the Sultan – that he hadn't stopped to consider what it might cost him.

"Did you tamper with it?" the Vizier pressed on, his voice now carrying a punch.

"If you have something to reveal to me, now is the time. I will know, of course, but I offer you a chance."

Did the Vizier know something already? Or was he simply bluffing to deceive Hassan?

"If you speak now, I can still set things right." He rose slowly, turning his back to Hassan as he spoke.

"Otherwise…"

He let the silence stretch.

"…There are consequences. You would be responsible for the failure of everything.

And I do mean… Everything." Hassan's thoughts spiralled. The pouch flashed before him; the plan he and

Zayd had put into motion, was it already lost? Was there still a way back? The room seemed to shrink around him, the pressure thickening with every breath. He could feel doubt creeping in – and with it, fear. The Vizier turned again, moving closer, perching lightly on the edge of the table as if he had all the time in the world.

"What is it, Hassan?"

"What is the truth?"

"Speak now, and I can help you. But delay…"

"And everything you are – and everything you might have been – will come crashing down."

Hassan shifted in his seat, sweat dampening his palms. The Vizier's words echoed louder than his own racing thoughts, pulling him in, pressing him towards confession. He opened his mouth – hesitated – the truth trembling on the edge of escape. The Vizier saw it. The flicker of uncertainty, the weakness – and struck with one final precision.

"Hassan," he whispered. "You have only one chance to tell me."

"Will you take it?" For a heartbeat, everything hung still – resting on the edge of ruin.

II

The silence felt strange, almost hollow. Zayd sat motionless in a quiet room of the palace, the faint creak of wooden beams above accentuating the stillness. His thoughts churned restlessly, the tension of the previous day refusing to loosen its grip. Through the open window, a faint breeze carried the muffled sounds of a waking city. A distant bray of a donkey broke the quiet, drawing his gaze towards the window. His mind wandered to the bustling streets of Al-Waadi, where farmers and labourers were already setting to work. He remembered watching them as a boy, preparing their donkeys for steep hills or uneven paths. The farmers would always cover the animals' eyes just before the climb. Once Zayd asked a farmer why. The man's answer had puzzled him at the time.

"It keeps them moving forward," the farmer said. "If they see the hill ahead, they'll stop. But cover their eyes, and they'll take it one step at a time."

The memory returned to him with vivid clarity. If fear could unmake the courage of men, why not the hearts of beasts? He remembered how the donkeys, seeing the steep climb ahead, would falter. Not from weakness, but from the enormity of the task before them. But when their eyes were covered, they focused only on the ground directly beneath their feet. The load on their backs remained the same; the hill was no less steep. Yet without the full climb pressing on their minds, they moved – not with certainty, but with enough resolve to reach the top. The thought lingered, carrying a quiet wisdom. Zayd leaned back, his gaze fixed on the open window. Perhaps, he too was at risk of being paralysed by the scale of the climb ahead. The path ahead felt impossibly steep – but maybe he didn't need to see the whole journey. With a slow exhale, he let the memory settle into him. Surrendering his fate to the will of the Almighty, Zayd returned to his duties in the palace. There was work to be done, and usually, the rhythm of it was enough to still his restless mind. But today, even the familiar motions could not banish the troubling questions swirling within him.

He thought of Hassan alone with the Vizier. The Vizier – a master of manipulation, weaving words into traps so subtly that one only realised too late they had been caught. And Hassan – bold, reckless, and easily swayed, his heart too quick to leap where his thoughts should linger. Could he stand against such a man? The questions tugged at Zayd, persistent and unwelcome. But he clung to the lesson he had found: the climb was not his to see all at once. Only the next step mattered.

"Zayd!" A voice broke through his thoughts.

He looked up to see Firas, one of the palace servants, hurrying towards him. His face flushed with a mix of excitement and urgency.

"What is it?" Zayd asked. Firas stopped just short of him, vibrating with the news.

"You've not heard?" he asked.

"Heard what?"

"The banquet," Firas said, his excitement spilling over.

"It's tonight, in the grand hall. And the guest of honour – they say it's a man who flew through the skies. Flown, Zayd!"

"Can you even imagine such a thing?"

Zayd froze.

Hassan.

There was no mistaking it. Perhaps the news of Hassan's flight had truly reached the Sultan, and he wished to hear the tale himself. But a more ominous thought surfaced. *What if this was part of the Vizier's plot? What if Hassan – wild and reckless – had become a stroke of fortune for him?* If Hassan had faltered under the Vizier's charm or pressure, if the truth about the seeds had slipped free, the consequences would be devastating. The Vizier would come for Zayd next – of that he was certain. And worse, if Hassan had been swayed, if he had betrayed their plan, the Vizier would simply adapt, scheming another way to strike at the Sultan. Zayd's mind churned with possibilities, each darker than the last. One thing was clear: he couldn't leave anything to chance. He had to ensure he was at the banquet, close enough to observe every detail. As head servant, he had enough sway to control the small details – who served what, who stood where. If the Vizier intended to act, Zayd needed to be ready. This wasn't about himself or Hassan anymore. The Sultan's life hung in the balance. And Zayd would see this through. Firas mistook Zayd's silence for awe.

"Amazing, isn't it?" he said, shaking his head.

"But come now, there's work to do. Best we get to it." He tapped Zayd on the shoulder and turned to leave.

"Firas, one moment," Zayd said, stopping him before he left.

"Tell me, if you see a stone lying in the road – a heavy one, one that others have passed by – do you stop to move it? Or do you also pass by another route?"

Firas stared, unsure of the nature of the question. He hesitated, as though considering his response, and then shrugged.

"If it is in my way, I move it."

The simplicity of the answer lingered as Firas walked away, leaving Zayd alone with his thoughts. It was unadorned, clear, and exactly what he needed. It is often the simplest answers that resonate most profoundly, Zayd realised.

If it is in my way, I move it.

Not for praise. Not to prove anything. But because it must be done. And perhaps, in that, lay the answer to his own struggle. Why should a man take on the burden's others have ignored? What compels him to step forward when the struggle is not his? It is not because he believes himself stronger or wiser. It is not because he seeks recognition. It is because the problem lies before him – and he sees it. Most will pass it by, telling themselves it is not their concern, not their duty. They turn away, hoping that someone else will come. But what if no one does? What if the road remains blocked, the danger unchallenged, the wrong unopposed? Zayd's heart ached with the enormity of it all. He thought of Hassan, alone with the Vizier. He thought of the seeds they had switched and the risk they had taken to thwart evil. And he thought of the doubt that gnawed at him now, urging him to step back, to let the world take its course without him. But Firas's simple answer whispered otherwise. The stone in the road might not be his – but it lay before him nonetheless. To walk past it would not make it disappear. And though moving it might strain him, might leave him scarred, he would know – deep within – that he had done what he could.

The burden is not chosen, Zayd realised. It is placed before you. And to act is not a matter of strength or certainty – it is a matter of will. For every man who steps forward, who dares to act for good, creates a ripple in the fabric of the world. His actions, small as they may seem, shift the balance. And though he may never see the full effect of his labour, the stone he moves today may clear the way for another tomorrow. The world does not change because of those who wait. It changes because of those who act. And Zayd knew, standing there in the quiet of the corridor, that his path had been laid before him. Whether Hassan faltered or stood firm, whether the Vizier's plans unravelled or adapted, Zayd would not turn away.

For if not him, then who?

III

As the purple hues draped the twilight sky, the royal banquet began, heralding a celebration of prosperity for the kingdom.

The grand hall sparkled with the warm glow of flickering candles that adorned lavishly set tables; their surfaces laden with exquisite delicacies. Joyful voices and laughter spilled into the air, carrying the essence of celebration. The Sultan and his esteemed guests settled in, eager for the night's entertainment. Jesters, poets, and storytellers were called forth one by one, weaving their magic with clever quips and enchanting tales. Among them stood Hassan, fidgeting nervously as he waited his turn. Servants darted about. Their movements swift and graceful, ensuring that every detail of the opulent affair ran seamlessly.

At the royal table, the Vizier sat beside the Sultan, a charming smile on his lips that masked his hidden anticipation. The candle flickering before him extinguished unexpectedly, a dark omen hinting at the sinister plot brewing beneath the surface of the festivities. As Hassan rose to share his story, the hall fell silent. Everyone turned to look at him with an expectant hush. The Vizier watched with an approving nod, though his attention remained partly elsewhere. Hassan's words poured forth, animated and lively, recounting his daring flight and the winds that had carried him to legend. He described the rush of the wind, the weightless exhilaration of defying gravity, and the courage it took to leap into the unknown. The audience was enthralled, leaning forward in their seats, gasping and laughing in all the right places. Cheers punctuated his pauses, and smiles spread across even the most guarded faces. But the Vizier? he had no time for such distractions. Waiting until the room seemed entirely absorbed in Hassan's tale before quietly, he rose from his chair. With a whispered excuse to the nobles seated beside him, he slipped away from the grand table, his departure unnoticed by the enraptured crowd.

This was the moment. The end of all his scheming; the culmination of his dark ambitions. Though a small man, he was filled to the brim with treachery. As he walked towards the kitchen, his mind stirred with the anticipation of the evil about to unfold.

This must be done, he thought, his focus sharpening.

Only a fool entrusts his destiny to lesser men. I trusted Zayd once – foolishly thinking his loyalty would suffice – but, he failed me. He faltered due to his carelessness. But I cannot afford such ruin, not when the mark is this close. I do not waste opportunity – I bend it. I take what I want, and the world has no say. No one sees the true weight I bear, he mused.

They call me loyal, wise, a servant of the Sultan – blind to the truth of what it takes to hold an empire together. To rule is not to play the saint. It is to manipulate, to deceive, to do what lesser men cannot stomach. They will never see as I see, never endure as I endure. Their hands are too clean, their hearts too soft. Only I have the will to do what must be done. As he neared the kitchen, a coldness gripped him, but it was nothing compared to the ice running through his veins.

Ruling demands sacrifice – not of oneself, but of those who stand in the way. If the price of the kingdom is a small sacrifice, then let it be paid. What the realm requires, I provide. Without mercy, without pause. Success is no whim or wish. It is destiny. His mind turned to the seeds nestled within the folds of his robe, their presence a reminder of both promise and consequence.

This act is not evil, he told himself for the hundredth time.

It is necessary. Does not the physician wield poison to cure the disease? Does not the fire burn the forest to make it fertile again? Power is not given. It is taken by those bold enough to claim it. Yet, even in his iron resolve, there lingered the faintest wisp of a question, almost imperceptible:

And if I am wrong?

He crushed it underfoot, unwilling to let doubt spoil the path he had chosen.

Evil is rarely born in a single moment. It begins as a whisper – a fleeting temptation, a justification planted deep within the heart. Left unchecked, it takes roots, wind-

A Parable of Fate | 143

ing through the soul, feeding on ambition, resentment, or fear. Yet an evil intention, un-acted upon, is not yet evil. It is merely potential. A seed, waiting for the right soil, the right moment to sprout into something more.

The true measure of a man lies not in the darkness he harbours, but in his will to confront it.

To choose restraint over indulgence. To wrestle with his darker impulses and emerge, if not untainted, then stronger for having resisted. It is a battle waged within, where victory is quiet, unnoticed, yet more profound than any triumph claimed in the world and beyond. But once evil is unleashed – once it steps beyond the boundary of thought into action – it becomes a force unto itself. A wildfire beyond the control of the one who sparked it. Like poison poured into the veins of a nation, it spreads, corrupting not only its source but all it touches. And with its release comes a heavy cost, for it is not only the world that suffers; the one who sets it free is bound irrevocably to its consequences. The threads of their fate intertwine with the harm they have shaped, drawing them ever closer to the ruin they believed themselves above.

The Vizier, of course, entertained no such doubts. To him, restraint was weakness. A trait of those too timid to act. He believed himself a necessary force, a sculptor carving order from chaos. But his ambition was the kindling, and his deeds were the flame. As he walked the path he had chosen, certain of its righteousness, the question remained unspoken: how long can you stoke such a fire before it consumes you too? For those who tread this path of evil, justification becomes a shroud, ambition a blindfold. They fail to see the simple truth – that what begins as a single dark thought, if nurtured, will eventually corrupt everything. And when that moment comes, the world will not wait for their redemption. It will swallow them whole, as surely as the flames they once believed themselves immune to.

Yet, in the heart of the chaos, a quiet truth remains:

Even the darkest fire can be doused. The most poisoned well can be cleansed. For while the poison of evil may course through the veins, the antidote of goodness can flow just as swiftly, restoring balance. A single thought – kindness, mercy, a fleeting moment of clarity – can begin the shift, like the first step taken on an untrodden path. The Vizier had yet to fully cross the line. He had not yet cast the first stone of his grand design, but the moment was near. He did not know it but for every dark path, a better way remains, waiting for those willing to seek it. Even in the midst of ruin, a single moment of reflection can halt the descent, for as long as there is breath in the body, there is a chance to set things right.

The Vizier entered the kitchen.

"You – out. All of you," he snapped.

The servants exchanged nervous glances but quickly obeyed, scurrying out in silence. The chef, still stirring a pot of stew, froze mid-motion. For a moment, he seemed unsure, his hand tightening around the spoon.

'I said all of you!' yelled the Vizier.

This left no argument and the chef abandoned his post and hurried out, leaving the stew unattended. The Vizier's gaze fixed on to the pot of stew simmering on the table, a rich aroma rising from it. He approached it slowly, his hand slipping into the folds of his robe, retrieving the pouch of seeds – his seeds. As he poured them into the bubbling stew, he tried to convince himself once more that this was an act for the greater good.

This is not treachery. This is devotion – true devotion. Allegiance to the kingdom of Al-Waadi. The Sultan's reign has stagnated, stalled in complacency. What is loyalty, if not the willingness to act when those in power fail? His thoughts, dark and sure, spun around him.

A kingdom does not thrive by sitting idle. The Sultan's reign is weak and I will be the one to correct it. I will be the one to lead. The kingdom will prosper through my hand. But as the steam rose from the pot, so too did the aroma of doubt. Perhaps it was his conscience arguing otherwise.

Is power worth it? his soul argued.

What is power, if it is built on betrayal and manipulation?

What good is a crown that is stained with the blood of those beneath it? Does it shine brighter when it is taken by force?

Power seized through betrayal, shattering the trust that binds a kingdom's soul, is but a fragile ambition, destined to unravel under its own strain.

The Vizier's hand trembled, but his resolve did not waver. He petitioned against his soul.

"I will not be weak. I will not be another man's shadow. I will take what is mine, and in time, they will see my greatness."

"This isn't self-destruction – this is my ascent!"

IV

*Just as the Vizier turned to leave, Zayd stormed into the kitch*en. Keen-sighted, he caught a faint glimpse of a pouch in the Vizier's hand before it disappeared into the folds of his robe. He had no proof, only instinct sharpened by desperation. What if Hassan had betrayed him? What if the Vizier had uncovered their plan and acted to salvage his own? What if...

The questions clawed at his resolve. He wasn't going to leave anything to chance. He was left with a choice:

stand aside and watch darkness take root, or confront it head-on.

"Well, well," the Vizier said, with an unnerving calm. "If it isn't the ever-dutiful servant…"

"Tell me, Zayd, what brings you here?"

"Brave of you, I must say, given how disappointed I am with your *recent failures.*"

Zayd stood tall. "Why did you send me to retrieve those seeds?"

"You knew they were poisoned, didn't you?"

The Vizier let out a soft chuckle, layered in contempt.

"I'm not going to let you do this," Zayd said, taking a step forward.

"Do what?" the Vizier asked, his pretend innocence tinged with mockery.

"Say it," Zayd snapped. "Say what you came here to do."

"You sent the staff away so you could tamper with the Sultan's food, didn't you?"

The Vizier's composure wavered, a flicker of shock crossing his face as Zayd stood firm. Zayd shifted his approach.

"You don't have to do this. You still have a choice. The damage has not yet been done, so don't let this be the path you take."

The Vizier's expression quickly darkened, nostrils flaring as if he could barely contain himself.

"Zayd, I will give you this advice once – and once only: know your place. You are a servant. Nothing more." His eyes burned with dark intensity and his words carried venom as he sought to reassert control, to intimidate Zayd back into submission.

"Yes, I will poison the Sultan. And no, you will not stop me. You pathetic, worthless boy."

Perhaps he believed Zayd to be insignificant, a mere servant whose defiance was laughable. Or perhaps his arrogance had grown so vast that he saw himself as untouchable, a force beyond challenge.

"The truth is, Zayd, men like you only serve to uphold the system, while men like me *shape* it. What you see as evil, I see as... necessary. You don't belong in matters like this. Yet you keep circling, louder, bolder – a fly begging to be crushed."

"Necessary?" Zayd spat.

"You think murdering the Sultan is necessary?"

"Oh, please. Spare me the moral outrage. Do you honestly believe a man like him – soft, blind to ambition – deserves the throne? The world doesn't reward goodness, Zayd. It rewards strength. And I will prove it!"

"You think betrayal is strength? Poison, ambition, lies – none of that will make you great." Zayd's voice grew louder, his fury burning through the room.

"You're not shaping the kingdom. You're destroying it!"

The Vizier pushed past him to leave, arrogance radiating from him.

"You overestimate yourself, boy."

"You are nothing."

Zayd's rage boiled over. With a roar, he lunged, slamming the Vizier and sending them both into a table. Pots and ladles clattered to the floor. The Vizier thrashed, trying to break free, his polished composure shattered into panic as Zayd pinned him hard against the wood.

"Ha! This is rich," the Vizier taunted.

"What's your grand plan here, boy? Pin me down and yell for help? You think anyone in this palace would take your word over mine? There is no one you can tell. No force you can muster."

"You simply can't stop me."

Zayd's jaw clenched. "You're right. Maybe I can't."

"But I can hold you off until this night is over," he growled.

With a desperate surge he drove the Vizier, crashing into another table. The impact was thunderous, more dishes and utensils clattered to the ground as the wooden frame groaned under the force. The Vizier crumpled against the wreckage, his arrogance momentarily replaced by shock, his breath coming in shallow, uneven bursts.

"Help!" He bellowed. "Servants! Guards! Anyone! This lunatic is attacking me!"

Three servants burst in. With firm hands, they tore Zayd away. They stood guard between him and the Vizier. Their eyes flickered between them in stunned confusion.

"What in the world is going on here?" one of them gasped.

"He's lost his mind!" the Vizier cried, pointing with a trembling hand.

"This madman attacked me unprovoked!"

"That's a lie!" Zayd shouted. "He's going to poison the Sultan!"

The Vizier's patronizing tone returned, as smooth and venomous as ever.

"Poor Zayd. Driven mad by delusions. Jealousy perhaps, or guilt."

"It's tragic, really."

The servants exchanged uncertain glances. They knew Zayd. They knew the Vizier. One was loyal, the other was feared. Deep down, they wanted to believe Zayd – his desperation felt real, his integrity unshaken – but fear gripped them, silencing their voices. The thought of the Vizier's power loomed over them, and in that moment, it seemed safer to stay still than to challenge the man who controlled their fates.

"Our guests were hungry and waiting," the Vizier said, brushing off his robes.

"I came to the kitchen to see what was taking so long, only to be attacked by this madman. I don't have time to waste on him now, but rest assured, I will make sure he gets exactly what he deserves."

He turned to the servants. "Get him out of this kitchen."

They hesitated, then seized Zayd's arms. In their bones they felt it – he was right. But fear held them captive, and they dared not defy the Vizier openly.

"You," the Vizier commanded, pointing at a servant who had just entered, "take this stew directly to the Sultan. No hesitations, no detours, no delays."

"Then get the rest of the staff; begin serving food to our guests immediately."

As he moved to leave the kitchen, the Vizier paused beside Zayd, his face only inches away. His words came as a whisper laced with poison, meant for Zayd alone.

"You've lost," he sneered. "I've already won."

"All your dreams, your plans – they're nothing but ashes now. Once the Sultan falls, you'll be the first to follow. Your days in this palace, your miserable little existence... they're finished."

He turned and left without looking back.

Zayd ripped his arms free from the servants' grip.

"Really?" He said, stepping back. "Are you seriously going to force me out? I work for the Sultan, not for that wicked man."

Zayd's shoulders sagged. He sank onto the nearest chair, burying his head in his hands. The bitter taste of defeat left him frustrated. *You thought you could stop this*, a cruel voice whispered in his mind. *Not a hero. Not a saviour. Just a servant, reaching beyond his place.* And for a moment, he believed it. His limbs felt heavy; his thoughts darkened. He thought of Al-Waadi, the guests, the poisoned stew heading for the Sultan. He had tried. He had fought. And still, it wasn't enough. Perhaps this is it, Zayd thought bitterly. Maybe the Vizier was right. The world wasn't shaped by good men. Virtue changed nothing. Their place was to serve, not to challenge. To uphold the order, not to rewrite it. But then, something stirred within him.

No.

If a man like the Vizier can be bold enough to seize power through evil, why can't I fight for good with the same fire? If ambition can be twisted, why can't purpose fuel a greater cause? He lifted his head. His fists curled at his sides. If one man's betrayal can shake a kingdom, then one man's courage can steady it. The world doesn't need more men like the Vizier – men who take and destroy. It needs men who stand, who refuse to yield, even when they falter.

And I will stand.

Because failure is not the end, but the crucible in which true strength is forged. A hero isn't born from triumph, but from the refusal to break, to stand time and time again, no matter how dark the hour. This isn't over.

Not tonight.

Not ever.

V

The banquet hall erupted in applause as Hassan's story reached its triumphant conclusion. The Sultan, seated at the head of the grand table, leaned back with a look of genuine delight. His hands came together in a rhythmic clap, his deep voice resonating through the hall.

"Magnificent, Hassan!" he declared.

"You have shown the spirit of Al-Waadi – how its people can reach heights that inspire us all. Truly, a better story has never been told in this hall."

The courtiers and guests echoed the Sultan's enthusiasm. Laughter rang out, mingling with the clinking of glasses and murmured exclamations of amazement. Hassan, flushed with pride but ever humble, offered a gracious bow. As he straightened, he stepped back into the crowd of entertainers, who greeted him with wide grins and murmured words of admiration.

At the head of the grand table, the Vizier rose, his presence commanding the attention of the room. His dark robes seemed to absorb the light. He raised his hands in a gesture of command, and with that the murmurs ceased.

"Ah, such stories, such artistry," he began. "Tonight, we celebrate not just the gift of words, but the power they hold. The power to build legacies, to inspire nations, to shape destiny itself."

Hassan was still aglow from the admiration showered upon him, when a figure emerged beside him.

Zayd.

Every inch of his stance spoke of purpose; his presence firm and unmistakable.

"Hassan. Look at me"

Hassan turned, still basking in the warmth of his thoughts. The moment he saw Zayd, his smile faded.

"I don't know where you stand anymore," Zayd whispered with urgency.

"Maybe the Vizier got to you. Maybe he twisted your pride, fed you his lies, and turned you. I don't know." He leaned in closer. "But if there's even a shred of the man I trusted left – then listen."

Hassan opened his mouth to respond, but Zayd didn't wait.

"This isn't about what we planned anymore. It's happening. Right now. The Vizier's plate – the stew they've just served him – it's poisoned."

Hassan blinked.

"I used the seeds," Zayd continued. "The real ones. The ones we were meant to throw away after we switched them in the pouch. I kept them. I don't know why, but something in me told me not to let go. I prayed I wouldn't need them."

He drew in a sharp breath, his conviction tempered by the faintest tremor of remorse, "but I did. I used them. So, one way or another, the Vizier will taste what he meant for the Sultan."

He hesitated, then added, "but I don't know if our switch even mattered. If you told him – if he figured it out

– he could've undone everything. He could still poison the Sultan and no one would know until it's too late."

His eyes searched Hassan's face, desperate.

"Did you tell him? Hassan, please – did you say anything? The Sultan's life depends on it."

He steadied himself. "Whether or not we succeed tonight, I swear I will not let the Vizier win. His schemes end here. One way or another."

For a moment, Hassan said nothing. Then, a broad smile took over his face.

"Zayd, my friend, what do you take me for?"

He shook his head gently.

"Yes, I'm old – maybe a little absurd – but a traitor?" He scoffed. "Never."

"The Vizier tried – oh, how he tried. Whispered threats. Promised riches. Tried to charm me, even played on my pride. He thought he could outwit me."

Hassan placed a firm hand on Zayd's shoulder.

"But he underestimated this old fool. I told him nothing. Not a single word."

"So, we – ?" Zayd said, searching.

"We're still in this together, my friend," Hassan said, cutting him off with a grin. He gave Zayd's shoulder a firm shake, not just to steady him, but to reassure him. "You didn't lose me."

His grin turned sly, almost mischievous. "But you're right about one thing – we can't let that treacherous fool walk away untouched. Let him taste every drop of the poison he brewed."

"This isn't about vengeance or clever games, Hassan. It's about the Sultan's life and the future of this kingdom."

He glanced towards the head of the hall. "The Vizier knows I'm onto him. If he spots me here, I won't make it ten paces before he has the guards drag me out. That's why I need you. Your voice, your charm – use them. Distract him, shake him. I can't do this alone."

He stepped closer. "Whatever it takes, we end this tonight."

Meanwhile, the Vizier's words rose in intensity, filling the hall with his inflated proclamations.

"Tonight, we gather not just to feast, but to reflect on the greatness of Al-Waadi. We celebrate not only the Sultan's reign, but the triumph of this kingdom – a kingdom that stands tall amidst the storms that seek to tear it down. For what is Al-Waadi, if not a testament to strength and resilience? It is a beacon in this turbulent world."

He moved with deliberate slowness, each step measured, his dark robes trailing softly behind him. As he approached the Sultan, he placed a hand on the ruler's shoulder. A gesture calm yet heavy with intent.

"We stand here because those who came before us understood that prosperity is not a thing of birthright – it is forged, it is earned. And though the Sultan's leadership has been vital, let us not forget the unseen hands that guide this kingdom. The ones who ensure its triumphs from the shadows."

"It is easy to be seen when victory is claimed, but it is harder still to be the one who quietly ensures the wheels of power keep turning." He paused, his eyes dipped briefly, as though his own words had unearthed a deep, unspoken thought.

"Our kingdom's true strength lies not only in its warriors, not in its conquests, but in those who understand that true power is cultivated, that it is built, brick by brick. And tonight, as we sit here among friends and allies, let us honour, in thought and word, those whose labour goes uncelebrated, whose wisdom is quiet but immeasurable. To the unseen architects of Al-Waadi's future."

He cast a measured glance at the Sultan, his eyes narrowing. Why wasn't the Sultan eating? Perhaps he needed a subtle nudge – enough to ensure he tasted the stew. With a faint smile that masked his intent, he continued...

"I would be remiss, of course, not to express our thanks to those who made tonight possible – the servants, the cooks, the very hands that have brought us this marvellous feast. To the chefs who crafted this meal, to those who ensured every detail was perfect, we owe our thanks. This is no ordinary banquet – it is a symbol of what Al-Waadi can achieve when its people work together, when we all play our part in this great machine."

"And with that, I – "

Hassan called out.

"Ah! But how would you know how delicious it is, Vizier? You're the only one who hasn't touched your plate!"

Laughter burst through the room like a gust of wind, growing louder as it spread. The Vizier's fingers twitched at his side. His expression remained a practiced picture of calm. His eyes scanned the room sharply. Who would dare interrupt the Vizier? His influence was extensive; his power absolute. Astonished faces turned towards the bold interrupter. Whispers broke out, hushed and urgent, disbelief threading through the gathered guests. Who would risk such audacity in the presence of both the Vizier and the Sultan? For a heartbeat, the Vizier's hand hovered over his plate, frozen in that uncomfortable pause. He hadn't expected this. Not here. Not in the Sultan's presence. His mask of charm slipped for a split second, the sharp edge of irritation creeping through. He was never caught off guard, never the one to falter in front of an audience. And yet, here he was, trying to regain control, to smooth over the disruption. Under different circumstances, the Vizier would have answered with cutting words, a masterful blend of disdain and authority that left no room for defiance. His sharp tongue had subdued greater challenges than this. But not tonight.

Tonight, everything was balanced on the edge of a blade. His plan was in motion, delicate and irreversible. He couldn't afford even the faintest crack in his composure, not a whisper of suspicion. Not now, when a single misplaced word might unravel everything. He swallowed his pride. Forced a smile. The Vizier turned towards the source of the interruption, his composure slipping as his gaze searched the room, trying to pinpoint the audacious fool who dared disrupt him.

"Ah, a jest, my friend," he said with a forced laugh.

"Just for you then…"

Silence followed.

The seconds crawled, thick with scrutiny. The room hung in this unnatural stillness, each moment stretching on with a suffocating intensity. He had always prided himself on his ability to remain unshaken, to move with the effortless grace of one who had mastered his own destiny. But that single heckle cracked the calm he projected. But why? What had changed in this instant to make the unshakeable Vizier sweat? The seeds. The poison. The Sultan's stew. He had played every angle, sealed every crack. Victory was inevitable. But instead, the silence fed uncertainty.

What if...

What if the poison hadn't worked?

What if the seeds had been switched?

What if they were now in his bowl?

For the first time, it felt as if he was no longer writing the script of his own fate. The very thought sent a chill through him. His stomach turned. He glanced down at his own plate, the stew before him seemingly unchanged. The thought was absurd, but it wouldn't leave him. *Could it be? Could Zayd have – ? Impossible. No. Focus. But should I take a bite? If I don't... will they notice? Will they wonder why? Will it look like I knew something was wrong?* He had to think clearly.

Surely the Sultan had taken a bite by now. It was only a matter of time. And yet, he couldn't shake that persistent whisper. This heckle – this foolish, irrelevant interruption – had thrown him into chaos. Do nothing, and suspicion grows. Refuse to eat, and it festers. And if the Sultan collapsed right here, right now, what would that look like? The assembly won't wait to judge.

"Perhaps the Vizier knew about the poison; that's why he didn't eat," they would say.

No.

He couldn't afford that. In a quieter corner of his mind, another thought played like a bitter symphony.

What if everything falls apart now?

What if he has been outwitted?

What if this is the end of the dream he built in the shadows?

His mind spun for a way out. His pride urged him to remain still, above it all. But instinct – honed from years of scheming – knew better: play the part. Keep the illusion. The crowd waited, expectant. He could feel their gaze, hot and heavy, pressing down on him. They wanted something.

Am I overthinking this? What do they want from me? A show of power? A demonstration of control? He could hear the unspoken command: *eat, or be exposed.* He lifted the spoon. The moment hung there, suspended, like the first drop of rain before a storm. He was no longer thinking of the poison, or the intricacies of his plan. He was thinking only of the reaction that would come when he failed to play his part, when he failed to mask the uncertainty. And yet, what choice did he have now?

The spoon touched his lips.

VI

"Mmm," the Vizier murmured with a forced calm as he strug-
gled to maintain his charming facade.

"Superb."

The spoon hovered, then dipped back into the bowl.
The clink of metal rang louder than it should have in the
sudden hush. He let the taste linger on his tongue, crafting each motion to project control – an illusion draped
perfectly over the chaos beneath. His eyes flicked back towards the shadowed corner where the heckle had come
from. It was pure performance – measured, casual, part of
the act. A glance to show confidence. To assure the room
he had nothing to hide. To satisfy the one who had called
him out. But something snagged. A twinge of doubt rip-
pled through his carefully composed exterior. Something
gnawed at the edges of his mind, refusing to be dismissed.
He drew in a breath.

Then he saw them.

Zayd and Hassan, standing together. Still. Determined.
Staring. The Vizier's stomach turned – not from the stew,
but from the dawning horror that consumed him. His eyes
widened, disbelief breaking through the mask he had so
meticulously constructed. Something had gone wrong.

Very wrong.

It was as if the air had been sucked from the room. Of course. Of course, they would have tampered with the stew. Zayd, that insufferable servant, had seen through him. He had ruined everything. His pulse thundered in his ears. For a fleeting moment, he felt suspended, caught between fury and dread. His mind raced, grasping for an explanation, a way to salvage the wreckage of his scheme. But no – the truth of it burned in their quiet defiance, in the way they met his gaze with unwavering resolve. The Vizier's breath hitched in his throat, a knot of panic tightening deep in his chest as the truth began to unfurl, slow and deceptive. His hand, once steady, trembled against the table, its grip faltering before it slid off the edge, like a final surrender. His eyes dropped to the bowl before him. He saw the seeds floating now, no longer the symbol of his triumph, but a damning reflection of his demise. The bite he'd taken, every moment of his self-assurance, now felt like a misstep on the path to his own undoing. A sickening thought tore through him – *Oh, no. What have I done?*

An oppressive heat radiated through his skin. His hand shot to his forehead, wiping away the torrent of sweat, but it only seemed to worsen the burning sensation creeping beneath his flesh.

"No," he whispered.

Then the cough came. A violent, ragged eruption that tore through his composure. He fumbled for his water, desperate to calm the growing panic inside him, but as he lifted the glass, his trembling fingers failed him. It slipped from his grasp; the dismay inside him had surfaced. The guests watched in stunned confusion, unable to comprehend what was happening. Another cough racked his body, followed by a searing pain in his chest.

"This can't be."

He clutched the edge of the table, rising shakily to his feet. His voice broke through the murmurs, raw and desperate.

"You..." he rasped, pointing at Zayd with a shaking hand. "You did this... how?"

Zayd's stillness carried an unrelenting pressure, a silent judgment that lingered above the Vizier like an executioner's raised hand. The Vizier now shifted his attention to Hassan.

"And you – you told me the pouch had not been tampered with." His words stumbled, a mix of fury and disbelief spilling out in the midst of his agony.

"I did, didn't I?" Hassan responded.

"Sometimes, Vizier, it's not what you overlook – it's who."

The words hit like a hammer. The Vizier's grip on reality began to splinter. He spun to face the Sultan.

"It was for you," he choked out.

"The poison – it was meant for you! I – I did it for Al-Waadi."

A collective gasp swept the hall, the Sultan's face frozen in disbelief. The Vizier turned back to Zayd, desperation flickering in his eyes.

"You don't understand! You couldn't. The Sultan – he's too blind, too soft. I am – "

" – You are a liar," Zayd interrupted, making his way forward.

"You used the kingdom as your excuse, but it was never about Al-Waadi. It was always about you."

The Vizier snarled, his fury overpowering his fading strength. With a sudden burst of energy, he lunged in the direction of Zayd, his hands clawing for his throat. But the poison was merciless. His legs buckled mid-swing, sending him crashing to the ground. He struggled to rise, his hands flailing against the floor, seeking something – anything – to hold onto, but his strength failed him.

He was crawling now, dragging himself forward with trembling arms. The man who once towered over the court like an unassailable fortress was reduced to this. A figure of pitiful desperation, face pressed against the cold stone, his breaths ragged and uneven. He looked up, his vision blurring. His gaze landed on Zayd, and his cracked lips twisted into something between a snarl and a plea.

"I... could have ruled the world," he gasped.

"Everything... within my grasp."

Zayd stepped closer, his shadow falling over the crumpled figure.

"And yet, you die here. Power was never yours to take – it was borrowed, stolen.

And now, it leaves you."

The Vizier reached, grasping for something, anything. But there was nothing left. There was no grandeur in his last moments, no final flare of glory, no heroic last stand. Instead, there was an oppressive stillness, a profound silence that swallowed the hall. His soul questioned:

What had it all been for?

The schemes, the lies, the throne he thought he could seize, the power he believed he deserved. It all seemed so small now, so distant. The lives he had ruined, the innocents trampled beneath his ambition – was it worth it? A low, bitter laugh bubbled from his chest, but it was more a rasping cough than a sound of triumph.

"I thought I was building something... something that mattered," he whispered to himself, barely able to breathe. "All for nothing."

He had spent his life constructing walls of deception, but in the end, it was not the world that had brought him down; it was his own hand that had pulled the foundation out from under him. He believed he was above it all, that he could outsmart everyone, even fate itself. But now, in the cold embrace of death, he knew: there had been no escaping this. What a waste. What an empty, hollow pursuit it had all been. The power, the influence, it had all been an illusion.

His breaths grew shallow. His fists unclenched. He lay there. Still. Crumpled. His final breath a fleeting sigh. The once-formidable figure of the Vizier, who had ruled the court with a sharp tongue and an iron will, was now reduced to nothing more than a body on the floor. His eyes, vacant and lifeless, stared at nothing, as though the world had lost all meaning in the space between one breath and the next.

VII

The hall hung in stunned paralysis. Courtiers glanced at one another, their expressions a mix of unease and disbelief. Some shifted uncomfortably, while others remained rigid, caught in the shock of the moment. The Vizier's body lay sprawled across the marble floor, an ugly testament to a night gone horribly wrong.

What does it mean to be betrayed by the very person you trusted most? The Sultan's heart ached with the pain of that question. The Vizier had been more than an advisor; he was a confidant, a friend – until he turned into an enemy lurking in the shadows. Do we invite betrayal by refusing to see the cracks in those we love? The guards hesitated, their movements uncertain as they stepped towards Zayd and Hassan. Their sense of duty clashed with the turmoil of what they had just witnessed. The man they typically obeyed had conspired against the very Sultan they were meant to protect.

"What do we do?" one of them muttered. Another guard, usually steadfast and composed, gripped his hilt tightly, casting an uneasy glance at his comrades.

"They killed him," another said, though the words lacked conviction.

Despite their training, this wasn't a scenario they had ever prepared for. They had trained for battles against foes clad in armour, not against betrayal from within their own ranks. Hassan stepped forward, hands raised in a mock surrender.

"Easy, my friends," he said. "I assure you. This isn't as bad as it looks."

"Not as bad?" a guard snapped. "The Vizier is dead from poison, and you dare to treat this lightly?"

Zayd moved between them, arms spread, voice firm.

"Hold your blades, all of you!" he urged.

"Let me speak to the Sultan."

All eyes turned. The Sultan sat motionless and hollow. The sting of betrayal pierced him like a dagger, his usual commanding presence subdued by disbelief. After a breathless pause, he raised a hand, granting Zayd the floor.

"Respected Sultan, this was not a night I ever wanted. Not a choice I relished. But it was one I had to make – for you, for Al-Waadi, for everything the Vizier sought to destroy."

As the Sultan listened to Zayd, he wrestled with the painful reality that trust, once broken, leaves scars that may never fully heal. In that moment, he recognised that the darkness of betrayal can illuminate hidden truths, revealing not only the flaws of others, but also the vulnerabilities within ourselves.

"The Vizier," Zayd gestured to the lifeless form, "was a man of shadows, a schemer who thrived on deceit and poison."

"Tonight, he planned to end your life with seeds laced in poison." He pointed to the table. "But the poison meant for you found its way to his plate instead."

"Do you know why?"

"Because the Vizier underestimated the people beneath him. He believed he could orchestrate his schemes without consequence. In his arrogance, he saw only his own cunning and failed to recognise the resolve of others."

"I did not bring the poison to this hall. The Vizier did. I did not conspire to betray you. He did. All I did was ensure that his wickedness consumed him...before it could consume you."

Hassan, ever the opportunist, spoke up. "Not the smoothest voyage, perhaps...but the ship still stands."

Zayd continued, feeling a growing apprehension due to the Sultan's silence.

"You placed your trust in him, respected Sultan, as we all did. He exploited that trust for his own gain. Saw us as tools to further his ambitions. But tonight, we stood for something better, for Al-Waadi. For you."

The Sultan's expression shifted, the impact of Zayd's words settling over him like a shroud.

"I had to act," Zayd said. "Because to do nothing would have been to betray you myself.

And that, I could never bear."

The Sultan slowly rose.

He surveyed the room, noting the astonished faces of the courtiers and the guards.

"You say the Vizier brought this poison here?"

"Yes, respected Sultan," Zayd replied.

"And you, Zayd… you saw it fit to end him, to save me?"

"I did what I thought was right. If I have erred, let my life pay the price."

The Sultan looked down at the corpse of the Vizier. His thoughts raced – memories of trust, of shared plans, the man he once called brother. *In a world where trust can be a weapon, who can we truly rely on?* He stroked his beard whilst calculating a verdict.

"You did not err," the Sultan said finally.

"You acted with courage, with loyalty, with love for this kingdom." He turned to the guards. "Stand down."

The guards wasted no time complying; the Sultan approached Zayd.

"You have given me the truth when others gave me lies. You risked your life when others plotted. For that… I thank you."

He looked to Hassan, who instinctively straightened in respect.

"And you. Though your methods may be unconventional, your loyalty shines through. This kingdom owes you both a debt."

He gathered himself, throat tightening, holding back the ache in his chest.

"You dreamed of the skies, Hassan – and in your own way, you soared. But never forget this: the beauty of life isn't in how high you fly… it's in knowing why you move at all."

He paused, as if carefully selecting the right words for Hassan.

"Fulfil your duty, see clearly the purpose behind your steps, and I promise you, that clarity will take you further than flight ever could."

Hassan placed a hand on his chest and bowed. For once, he found no words. The Sultan allowed himself a faint smile before his expression grew solemn once more.

"Tonight, we've seen the worst of humanity – greed, betrayal, deceit. But we've also seen its best – loyalty, courage, sacrifice. Let us never forget either."

With that, the Sultan turned and walked from the hall, his robes flowing behind him, leaving the court to process the storm that had just passed. As the murmurs rose in the wake of his departure, Hassan patted Zayd's back.

"Well, my friend, I think that went rather well."

Zayd allowed himself a small smile. "For once, Hassan... you may be right."

The court began to shift, the atmosphere changing from shock to quiet admiration. Whispers of their heroics spread like wildfire, and soon, the two men found themselves surrounded by nods of approval, grateful smiles, and murmured thanks. Heroes, they were called. And though the night had been dark and fraught with peril, the dawn that followed would remember them as such.

VIII

The stars over Al-Waadi had never looked brighter. Perhaps it was the clarity of the night after the storm, or it was simply the feeling – that the future, once so clouded by uncertainty, now shimmered with possibility. For Zayd, the night was a paradox: quiet in its calm, yet roaring in memory. Everything that had happened still echoed through him. He thought of his earliest days –

A young man brimming with dreams, his heart set on becoming a judge. Back then, he believed that justice was his calling – a clear and noble path to walk. But the twists and turns of life had taught him that fate rarely walked in straight lines. His journey had been anything but linear:

from humiliation to triumph, from doubt to belief, from servant to hero. What he hadn't understood then was that the trials, the heartbreaks, the moments of despair, had not been diversions from his path. They had been the path itself. Each stumble had sharpened his resolve. Every failure had expanded his vision. And in the end, he had not merely become a judge –

He had become the Vizier, a position that bore not just the responsibility of justice, but the weight of guiding a kingdom. This journey was not about predicting what lay ahead. It was about trusting that every twist, every turn, every detour carried meaning. Fate is not a straight road, but a winding story, rich with lessons if you are willing to read between the lines.

And what of Hassan?

Hassan's dreams had seemed as wild and untamed as the man himself –

A dreamer with eyes on the skies, a tinkerer who saw possibilities where others saw madness. Yet now, Hassan's name would be etched in the history of Al-Waadi, not just the first man to fly, but as the man whose courage and ingenuity had saved his kingdom from treachery. Hassan had shown that dreams, no matter how far-fetched, could take flight if one dared to pursue them.

Zayd leaned back in the soft cushions of Hassan's home. The scent of spiced tea and freshly baked bread curled in the air. Laughter filled the room, warm and unrestrained. It wasn't the laughter of a guest trying to be polite, but of someone who belonged, someone at ease.

"Zayd," Yasmin said, her voice teasing, "how is it that you've been here so often, I'm starting to think you've forgotten your own house?"

Zayd grinned, holding up his tea. "Why would I leave when the hospitality is this good? Hassan's cooking alone keeps me anchored."

"Cooking?" Hassan interjected, feigning offense. "You think I've been in the kitchen? That's my wife's doing. All I do is eat – and even that I do better than you."

They burst into laughter. Zayd shook his head.

"You're right, Hassan. You're unmatched in your ability to consume food. Truly a talent for the ages."

Yasmin rolled her eyes. "You two are impossible."

"That's what makes us brilliant," Hassan joked, leaning back with a satisfied sigh. "Are we not brilliant, Zayd? The kingdom owes us a feast every night for what we've done."

Zayd's laughter softened into a smile. "We haven't earned anything, my friend. We just fulfilled our duty."

Before the conversation could deepen, the door creaked open, and a guard stepped in. His armour gleamed in the lantern light, his presence a reminder of the world outside.

"Respected Vizier," the guard said with a respectful nod, "the Sultan requires your presence at the palace."

The room stilled. Yasmin's eyes flicked to Zayd, pride and admiration in her gaze. Hassan, however, simply grinned.

"Well, Vizier," he said, the title rolling off his tongue with mocking grandeur.

"It seems duty calls again. Don't forget to mention my contributions to the Sultan. Maybe he'll name me Chief Inventor or something."

Zayd laughed and stood. He patted Hassan on the shoulder.

"If I know you, you'll have invented a grander title by the time I return."

IX

As Zayd stepped into the cool embrace of the night, his thoughts drifted to the winding journey that had brought him here. This was his parable – a parable of fate, of steps uncertain and paths uncharted. How often had he questioned the turns his life had taken, doubted the stillness of those moments when it felt as though he were treading water? In those times, he had cursed the quiet, mistaking it for stagnation. He had wrestled with the uncertainties of his path, yearning for clarity, demanding answers to the how and why. But now, standing as Vizier, he saw the pattern. Every dull hour, every seemingly futile task, every crushing doubt. Each hardship had acted like a careful polish, revealing the brilliance hidden beneath the surface. The emptiness had not been a void, but a preparation. The stillness, a moment of rest, revitalising him for the battles ahead. It was never about trusting fate blindly; it was about trusting the process –

About believing that the smallest, most mundane steps mattered. Every hesitation, every leap, every fall had led him to this moment, where his hands could shape the future. The night stretched endlessly above him – vast and unknowable. But for the first time, Zayd embraced it. All that had ever been required of him was to take the next step –

And to act when it mattered. In that moment, beneath the vast sky, he understood:

Destiny is not something to await. It is something to create.

There's a quiet misunderstanding in the way people see others who have reached some semblance of peace or success. They see the calm waters and assume there were never storms. They see the sturdy tree and forget it was once a fragile sapling, bent and battered by the winds. But no one becomes whole without first breaking.

No one ascends without first climbing –

Calloused hands gripping the edges of hope, slipping often, but refusing to let go.

What you see now –

The resilience, the wisdom, the poise –

Is not a denial of struggle. It is a culmination.

It's tempting to believe that the strong cannot understand the weak, that the healed cannot comprehend the wounded. But strength is forged in the fire of hardship. The one who walks steady today once stumbled, bruised, and crawled. The scars they carry are not erased. They are simply worn differently –

Proudly, quietly, as testaments to battles fought and lessons learned.

Yet, here lies the beauty: those who have endured the hardest trials rarely flaunt their pain. They do not measure their worth by their suffering. Instead, they walk with gratitude –

For what they've gained, for the grace that carried them when their own strength faltered. They know that hardship, while painful, was also a teacher. Perhaps the lesson then, is this: do not judge the present by the absence of the past. The serene face you see may hide stories of chaos. The success you admire may be the fruit of silent, unseen toil. And the calm voice offering you advice may once have trembled with uncertainty. Let it inspire, not alienate. Let it remind you that your own struggles, no matter how heavy they feel, are shaping you in ways you cannot yet see. And when you reach your own summit – because you will – remember:

The strength you've earned does not separate you from others. It connects you to them.

The story of every victory is not one of ease –

But of endurance.

So, endure.

And when someone admires the calm of your waters, let it remind you of how fiercely you once fought the storm.

About the Author

Ibtesam Ismail is a management consultant from Manchester, UK, who writes simply for the joy of it. He developed a love for short stories and the hidden magic of storytelling over time, drawn to the way words can play, surprise, and linger.

His writing often leans whimsical at first glance, but look a little closer and you'll find layers of thought and meaning tucked between the lines. His debut novel, *A Parable of Fate*, is hopefully the first of many.

Printed in Dunstable, United Kingdom